BRAVE HIS SOUL

The Story of
Prince Madog of Wales
and His Discovery of
America in 1170

BRAVE HIS SOUL

By Ellen Pugh

WITH THE ASSISTANCE OF DAVID B. PUGH

DODD, MEAD & COMPANY
New York

5/81

FOR MY MOTHER

LLONGAU MADOG

Wele'n cychwyn dair ar ddeg
O longau bach ar fore teg:
Wele Madog ddewr ei fron
Yn gapten ar y llynges hon.
Mynd y mae i roi ei droed
Ar le na welodd dyn erioed:
Antur enbyd ydyw hon,
Ond Duw a'i deil o don i don.

Sêr y nos a haul y dydd
O gwmpas oll yn gwmpawd sydd:
Codai corwynt yn y De,
A chodai'r tonnau hyd y ne':
Aeth y llongau ar eu hynt
I grwydro'r môr ym mraich y gwynt.
Dodwyd hwy ar dramor draeth
I fyw a bod er gwell er gwaeth.

Wele'n glanio dair ar ddeg
O longau bach ar fore teg:
Llais y morwyr glywn yn glir
'R ôl blwydd o daith yn bloeddio 'Tir!'
Canent newydd gân ynghyd,
Ar newydd draeth y newydd fyd—
Wele heddwch i bob dyn
A phawb yn feister arno'i hun.

—Ceiriog
(John Hughes, 1832-1887)

THE SHIPS OF MADOG

Thirteen small ships did sail away
One morning long ago
With Madog, brave his soul and free,
As Captain of the fleet.
Resolved he was to set his foot
Where man had never trod;
An awful, fearsome venture this—
God keep him safe from harm!

The sun by day, the stars at night,
His only compass were.
Great hurricanes surged from the south
With waves that raked the sky;
The ships were tossed from off their course
As if a giant arm
Would shove them to the nothingness
That lay beyond earth's rim.

Thirteen small ships discovered land
One morning long ago.
The weary sailors cried with joy
And rushed upon the earth
They never thought to see again.
The Captain spread his arms—
"Behold here peace for every man,
And my long dream fulfilled!"

(Freely translated by Ellen Pugh)

 ACKNOWLEDGMENTS

THE WRITING OF A BOOK SUCH AS THIS, involving as it does the fitting together of myriad bits and pieces of information from several countries and over many centuries, could not possibly be accomplished without the aid and encouragement of many persons.

Thus, it is a pleasure to acknowledge the generous help of the staff of the beautiful Llyfrgell Genedlaethol Cymru (National Library of Wales) in Aberystwyth; Miss Megan Ellis, Keeper of Prints, Drawings and Maps, and Mr. Moelwyn I. Williams, Keeper of Printed Books, receive my especial thanks.

In this country, Mrs. Addison A. Mauldin, as executrix of the estate of the late Hatchett Chandler, Curator of Fort Morgan, Alabama, was very helpful, supplying information and photographs. Miss Christine I. Andrew, Senior Reference Librarian at Yale University, and Mrs. Goldena Howard, Reference Librarian at the State Historical Society of Missouri, in Columbia, aided me with a knotty bibliographical problem. Mrs. Howard, herself interested in the subject of the Welsh Indians, also provided me with some overlooked citations. Mr. Kinchen Exum, Associate Editor of the *Chattanooga News-Free Press* and administrator and residual legatee, *cum testamento annexo*, of the literary estate of the late Zella Armstrong, author of *Who Discovered America? The Amazing Story of Madog,* was most generous and helpful.

I am grateful to all who helped me locate and/or supplied me with the illustrative material. Chief among these are Mrs. Rebecca S. O'Neal, of the Department of Painting and Sculpture in the Smithsonian Institution's Collection of Fine Arts, and the staff of the Prints and Photographs Division of the Library of Congress in Washington, D.C. Dr. J. Leitch Wright, Jr., Associate Professor of History at Florida State University, in Tallahassee, gave needed information concerning the portrait of "General" Bowles.

Those who encouraged me are too numerous to cite, but one person must be named—my non-Welsh but enthusiastic editor at Dodd, Mead & Company, Joe Ann Daly. Her interest in this project sustained me through many frustrating hours, and I wish to express my appreciation publicly.

To any whom I have inadvertently omitted, my apologies—and my thanks.

—E.P.

 FOREWORD

ON NOVEMBER 10, 1953, THE
Virginia Cavalier Chapter of the Daughters of the American
Revolution erected a memorial tablet at Fort Morgan,
Mobile Bay, Alabama. The marker reads: "In memory of
Prince Madoc, a Welsh explorer, who landed on the shores
of Mobile Bay in 1170 and left behind, with the Indians,
the Welsh language."

Yet few Americans seem to have heard of this nobleman.
Columbus, our schoolbooks say, discovered America. In
1492. Everyone knows that.

Who, then, was this man, Prince Madog? (Or Madoc.)
Why do we think he landed in Mobile Bay so long ago?
And who were the Welsh Indians?

We know that an invention is often not the work of one
man. Thomas Edison, working in New Jersey, made a
phonograph in 1877. But so did Charles Cros, in France.
Earlier, in 1837, Samuel F. B. Morse invented the tele-
graph. That very year, Sir Charles Wheatstone and William
Fothergill Cooke, in England, patented an "electric tele-

graph." We study Darwin's theory of evolution, but Alfred Russel Wallace developed it about the same time. Cyrus McCormick operated his reaper in 1831, yet Obed Hussey received the earliest patent for one, in 1833. The courts had to decide whether Alexander Graham Bell or Elisha Gray first invented the telephone. The steamboat was made five times, by five different men, in five different places.

Need it be otherwise in geographical discovery? Columbus has the credit for reaching America, but how many—both known and unknown—preceded him?

It is eight hundred years since one of them, Madog, sailed. It is time we learned about him.

—ELLEN PUGH

Pullman, Washington

ILLUSTRATION CREDITS

Memorial erected at Mobile Bay. (Courtesy of Mrs. Addison A. Mauldin) PAGE xvi

Wales in 1100. (Reproduced with permission of Faber & Faber, Ltd., from *An Historical Atlas of Wales from Early to Modern Times* by William Rees) PAGE 7

Dolwyddelan Castle. (From an engraving by Samuel and Nathaniel Buck in 1742, with permission of The National Library of Wales) PAGE 13

Francis Lewis, painted by A. Rosenthal. (Independence National Historical Park Collection) PAGE 37

Iolo Morganwg. (By permission of The National Museum of Wales) PAGE 45, TOP

Another portrait of Iolo Morganwg. (From an etching by Robert Cruikshank of a drawing by Elijah Waring, with permission of The National Library of Wales) PAGE 45, BOTTOM

William Augustus Bowles. From an engraving of Thomas Hardy's portrait. PAGE 47

The Reverend Dr. Samuel Jones. (Courtesy of The Historical Society of Pennsylvania) PAGE 53, TOP

Thomas Jefferson, painted by James Sharples, Sr. (Independence National Historical Park Collection) PAGE 53, BOTTOM

Buffalo chase, single death. Painting by George Catlin. (Library of Congress) PAGE 62

Buffalo chase, with bows and arrows. Painting by George Catlin. (Courtesy of National Collection of Fine Arts, Smithsonian Institution) PAGE 63

A portion of John Evans' map. (Library of Congress) PAGE 67

William Clark, painted by Charles W. Peale. (Independence National Historical Park Collection) PAGE 79

CONTENTS

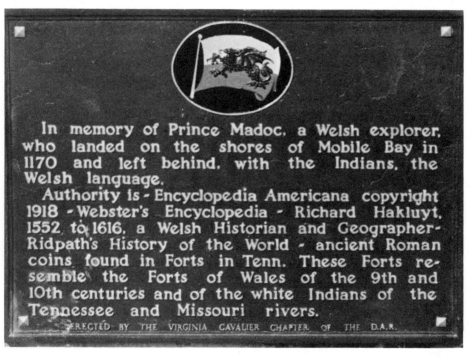

In memory of Prince Madoc, a Welsh explorer, who landed on the shores of Mobile Bay in 1170 and left behind, with the Indians, the Welsh language.

Authority is - Encyclopedia Americana copyright 1918 - Webster's Encyclopedia - Richard Hakluyt, 1552 to 1616, a Welsh Historian and Geographer- Ridpath's History of the World - ancient Roman coins found in Forts in Tenn. These Forts resemble the Forts of Wales of the 9th and 10th centuries and of the white Indians of the Tennessee and Missouri rivers.

ERECTED BY THE VIRGINIA CAVALIER CHAPTER OF THE D.A.R.

Memorial erected at Fort Morgan, on Mobile Bay, Alabama, by the Virginia Cavalier Chapter of the Daughters of the American Revolution in 1953

Prologue

MORE THAN THREE centuries before Christopher Columbus arrived in the New World, an obscure Welsh prince is believed to have landed in Mobile Bay.

There are several reasons for believing this, but the most compelling evidence lies in the frequent reports of English and French explorers of the late seventeenth, eighteenth, and early nineteenth centuries, saying that they met with Indians who were light-skinned, had beards, and spoke the Welsh language—descendants of Prince Madog and his followers.

Hearing these accounts, one Welshman came to America, from North Wales, just to search for his kinsmen, the Welsh Indians. He said he did not find them, but he may have lied—for Spanish gold. One of America's great but neglected artists, not looking for Welsh Indians, said he found them, and left us pictorial—and other—testimony.

The pages that follow set forth the evidence, pro and con, for Madog's voyage and the existence of the Welsh Indians. Was it all just myth or legend? Prince Madog *did* exist; a voyage *was* possible. But did it really take place?

1

 CHAPTER 1

A King Dies

IN WASHINGTON,
D.C., in the year 1801, Lt. Joseph Roberts, a Welshman
born in Hawarden, Flintshire, entered the formal dining
room of a hotel.

Seated at table, the officer ordered a brandy-and-water
to accompany his meal. He knew the young waiter to be
Welsh—presumably Roberts dined frequently at the un-
specified hotel—and when he was brought a drink containing warm water instead of cold, he spoke sharply to the
waiter, but in Welsh, so as not to embarrass him before
others.

Then, in Roberts' own words, "there happened to be in
the room at the time one of those secondary Indian chiefs,
who, on my pronouncing those words, rose in a great hurry,
stretching forth his hand, at the same time asking me in the
ancient British tongue, 'Is that thy language?'

"I answered him in the affirmative, shaking hands at the
same time, and the chief said it was likewise his language
and the language of his father and mother and of his nation.

"I said to him, 'It is also the language of my father and mother and also of my country.' Upon this, the Indian began to inquire from whence I came, and I replied, 'From Wales,' but he had never heard of such a place. I explained to him that Wales was a principality in the Kingdom called England. He had heard of England, but never of such a place as Wales."

The long chain of events that culminated in this and numerous other surprising encounters between early white settlers and explorers in America and Welsh-speaking, befeathered Indians, began many centuries earlier, in November of 1169, when Owain ap Gruffydd ap Cynan, King of Gwynedd (later the Principality of North Wales) died. And as the messengers rode out from Aberffraw, the ancient seat of Gwynedd's rulers, to spread the news throughout the kingdom, the wonder was not that Owain was dead but that he had died peacefully in his bed.

The turn of events, plus his own driving ambition to extend his realm, caused him to war constantly against other Welsh princes—many of them his kinsmen—as well as against the Anglo-Norman king, Henry II. This monarch, Henry II, finally—in 1165—after two temporary successes, gave up in despair his attempt to subject mountainous little Gwynedd to English rule. Then too, while a valiant leader and efficient administrator, Owain seems to have been even more ruthless than most rulers in that bloodthirsty time. Countless murders and barbarous mutilations—particularly of his relatives—are chronicled. He ordered his brother Cadwallon and his nephew Cunedda, among others, to be blinded and cruelly maimed. Surely such a brutal man,

living in a violent age, should have died on the battlefield
or been assassinated by any one of his many enemies.

Yet the last years of Owain's reign were spent quietly in
Aberffraw, marred only by a deepening of his long and
complicated struggle with the Church. He had by this time
married Crisiant, his first cousin; and for it he was excom-
municated by Thomas à Becket, Archbishop of Canterbury.
Owain was still under the ban when he died; however,
Welsh priests cheerfully ignored Canterbury's rulings, and
Owain received his church's sacraments. A few months
later, Becket relented and the dead king was interred before
the high altar of Bangor Cathedral, beside his brother Cad-
waladr with whom—in life—he had alternately warred and
allied.

Owain's several marriages had been of a casual and
irregular kind, common to the age and country, and few
of his numerous children were deemed legitimate by
churchmen. (He is said to have had seventeen sons and at
least two daughters; fourteen of these children are mentioned by name in the old Welsh chronicles.) In this confused situation, even before Owain died, bitter argument
arose among his surviving sons as to who could—and who
would—succeed him.

The oldest legitimate son, Iorwerth Drwyndwn, the
logical choice, had no claim. According to the Welsh laws
of the period, no one bearing a physical blemish could
reign: Iorwerth had a deep scar across his face, sustained
—some say—in a brawl with a kinsman. There are indica-
tions he was also feeble-minded. In any case, he quickly
withdrew to Dolwyddelan Castle, a second residence of

Owain, and seems not to have been heard from again.

Another son, Howel, something of a poet and with an Irish mother named Pyvog, seized the throne and held it precariously for two years. He then went to Ireland to claim his mother's property, a greedy but rather unintelligent act; for upon his return, he found his brother Dafydd firmly in control of Gwynedd. It is uncertain what happened to Howel. One source says he went back to Ireland; another, that he was killed by Dafydd's army.

But Dafydd was having his woes. For one thing, he had married Emma Plantagenet, sister of the hated English king, Henry II, against whom his father, Owain, had warred so long—and successfully. It was widely rumored that Dafydd had secretly supplied the despised Henry, now his brother-in-law, with a thousand men and money; and it was a known fact that he had attended a session of the English Parliament in Oxford. It was surmised that he had, while there, sworn allegiance to the English ruler. This was far more than even a tolerant Welshman—and they were few—could stomach. Uprisings became frequent, and Dafydd's supporters, many of them, now openly favored the disbarred Iorwerth. Fearful of losing his hold, Dafydd had these detractors murdered, and then confiscated their lands. Soon Gwynedd was held fast in a reign of terror. Frantic in his determination to keep the throne, Dafydd next imprisoned his brother Rhodri, a reluctant contender, and forced his other church-recognized brothers—Riryd, Edwall, and Einion—into exile.

Now there was no one to challenge him. But national discontent grew; Gwynedd engaged in a fierce and bloody civil war.

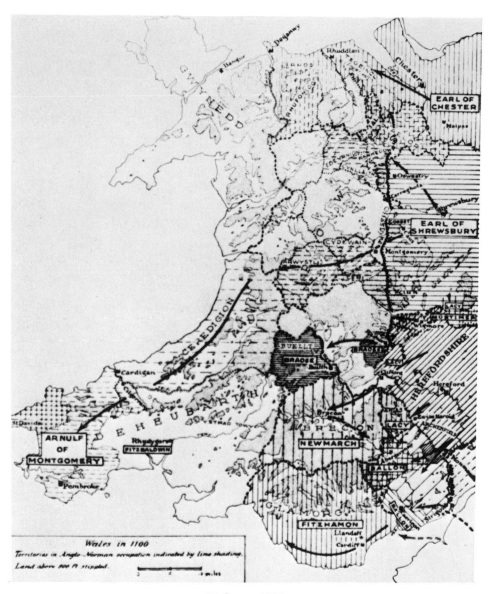

Wales in 1100

There was one son of Owain who looked on all this warfare and petty quarreling, and wished only to be far away
from it. Disgusted with the shameful strife all around him,
and before Dafydd could banish him, Madog, a handsome,
mild-mannered man, exiled himself at sea. And because of
bitter contention over the throne of far-off, tiny Gwynedd,
it is probable that America had a noble Welsh explorer on
her soil in 1170, over three hundred years before Columbus!

Of Madog's earliest years very little is known. It is likely
he was born at Dolwyddelan Castle rather than at Aberffraw, and that his mother was named Brenda, though there
is no positive contemporary evidence of this. There is a legend that Madog was born with a club foot and, according
to the old Welsh law, was to be put to death at once; and
that Brenda, seemingly acceeding to Owain's decree, had
her baby son secretly taken to Pendaran, an old Druid
known to her in her childhood. Pendaran raised the boy; and
the lad's identity was not revealed to Owain until Madog
was sixteen years old, when Brenda, on her deathbed, con-
fessed all. But this is legend, not substantiated fact.

Indeed, there are many scholars who consider Madog's
very existence, let alone his discovery of America, to be no
more than legend. Mainly, they base their argument on the
fact that Madog, a son of Owain, is not mentioned in the
oldest Welsh chronicles, the *Brut y Tywysogion* (*Chronicle
of the Princes*) and the *Annales Cambriae* (*Annals of Wales*)
or in any bardic poem of the time. The matter is further
confused by the fact that during this particular period of
Welsh history there were at least six men named Madog
whose deeds the chroniclers recorded.

It is frequently asserted that Madog's princely existence

was noted in the annals kept by the monks at the abbeys of
Ystrad Fflur (Strata Florida) and Conway. Perhaps so; but
very few of the records in Ystrad Fflur, founded in 1091 in
Cardiganshire, have come down to us. What of them do
remain were fully documented by a British historian in
1889, and there is no mention of Madog. And unfortunately,
when Edward I conquered Wales in 1282 and moved Conway Abbey to Maenen, many old records were destroyed
or lost.

However, documents do exist which seem to make it
clear that a natural son of Owain, named Madog, lived. In
an ancient Welsh manuscript in the Cottonian Collection
in the British Museum in London there is a long account
of the lineage of Gruffydd ap Cynan, citing him as the
father of Owain and grandfather of "Madawc." Also, a
Latin manuscript in this same collection, under the heading
Vita Griffini Regis (*The Life of King Gruffydd*), identifies
Gruffydd as the son of Cynan, and father of Owain, both
kings of Gwynedd, as is well known. But—it goes on to say
that Owain's son explored *unknown* lands.

This manuscript, referring to a Welsh explorer of unknown lands, is dated 1477, fifteen years before Columbus
sailed, and should effectively squash frequent claims that
not until after Columbus' achievement did British historians
and propagandists cite Madog's voyage—in a feeble attempt
to refute Spain's claim to have been the first nation to discover the New World.

The Welsh bards also took notice of Madog; the earliest
such mention of him known to us is in a poem by Maredudd
ap Rhys, a noted bard and clergyman of the mid-fifteenth
century:

Helied Ifan, hael dyfiad
Ar y tir teg, wedi'r tad;
Mewn awr dda minnau ar ddwr,
O fodd hael a fydd helwr—
Madog wych, mwyedig wedd
Iawn genau Owain Gwynedd
Ni fynnai dir, f'eniad oedd,
Na da mawr ond y moroedd.

Let Evan of generous growth hunt
Upon his fair land, his true patrimony;
In an auspicious hour, I also on water,
With the consent of the generous one, will be a hunter.
Madog am I, the son of Owain Gwynedd,
With stature large and comely grace adorned,
No lands at home, nor store of wealth me pleased,
My mind was whole to search the ocean seas.

In another ode, sometimes said to be only a distorted version of the one quoted above, Maredudd—who died thirty years before Columbus landed in America—is even more specific:

On a happy hour he is on the waters,
Of manners mild the hunter will be,
Madog brave, of pleasing countenance,
Of the true lineage of Owain Gwynedd,
He coveted not the land,
His ambition not great wealth
But the sea.

(It should be emphasized here that the bards of ancient Wales played a significant role in national affairs. Indeed, one of the most important officers of a Welsh king's—or nobleman's—court was the bard, whose duties were clearly defined. The chief of these was to record—in verses easy to memorize, and set to catchy tunes—events of concern to all the people. The bard also recorded the marriages, births, and deaths in the household of his patron, and prepared genealogies when required to establish lines of succession. The discovery of printing lay far in the future, so that the bard actually performed the function of a newspaper, a diary, or a journal. So important was this office that he was deemed a sacred personage, and his body was inviolable; to injure a bard was among the most heinous of crimes. A bard's songs, commemorating the notable events of his time, were handed down verbally from generation to generation; and it is obvious that very few of them survive to this day, though the priests of the abbeys—who alone could read and write—did occasionally put some of them down in Latin. But even these—almost all of them—were lost to us by 1284, with the aforementioned conquest of Wales and subsequent destruction of the monasteries.)

A minor Cardiganshire poet, Deio an Ieuan Du, writing about the same time as Maredudd ap Rhys, makes it clear in a long poem that by the fifteenth century Madog was almost a patron saint of Welsh fishermen, and renowned as a brave and skillful sailor. Two lines of the poem identify him as a son of Owain:

> fal Madog, marchog y medd,
> baun gwyn, fab Owain Gwynedd.
>
> like Madog, knight of the mead,
> fair peacock, son of Owain of Gwynedd.

In 1584, after the development of printing, Dr. David Powel published *The Historie of Cambria, Now Called Wales,* actually just a translation of Humphrey Llwyd's continuation of the *Brut y Tywysogion.* In it, Powel lists all of Owain's sons (Rhodri, Cynoric, Riryd, Meredydd, Edwall, Cynan, Rhum, Maelgwyn, Llewellyn, Iorwerth, Dafydd, Cadwallon, Howell, Cadell, Madog, Einion and Phylip) and says of Madog that he "left the land in contention between his brethren and prepared certain ships with men and munition, and sought adventures by seas, sailing west."

Later British historians, such as Richard Hakluyt in 1600 and Samuel Purchas in 1625, supported Powel, yet added little to his account of Madog's voyage. Finally, skipping a few centuries, the prestigious multi-volume *Dictionary of National Biography* includes Madog in its lives of distinguished Britons, though it cautiously refers to him as the "reputed" son of Owain Gwynedd.

Among American historians, Captain John Smith in 1621, William Hickling Prescott in 1843, and John Clark Ridpath in 1899, took due note of Madog, as did Benjamin F. De Costa, the authority on pre-Columbian voyages to America, in 1901.

These have all been Welsh, English—and a few American—evidences for Prince Madog's existence. Did any other European nation know of, or record, his voyage? Indeed so. We know that about 1255 Willem the Minstrel, living in Flanders, translated a long romance about Madog from the Welsh priests' Latin. Since this occurred only eighty-five years after Madog sailed, it would seem to prove that bardic songs had truly publicized the Welsh prince's accomplish-

Dolwyddelan Castle, supposed birthplace of Madog

ment throughout Wales. How did Willem get hold of the Latin version? Simple: in 1112, King Henry I of England had planted a colony of Flemish immigrants—weavers, mainly—along the English-Welsh border, after their low-lying country had been inundated by the sea, as a barrier against Welsh raids into English territory. The descendants of these colonists returned to Flanders in 1250, taking with them the Arthurian legends and bardic songs they had learned during their sojourn in Wales. (There is some evidence that Willem himself may have lived in Wales for a few years.)

A later Dutch scholar, Hornius, stated in his *De Originibus Americanis*, published at 's Gravenhage (The Hague) in 1652, that "Madoc, a Prince of Cambria [Wales], with some of his nation, discovered and inhabited some lands in the west, and that his name and memory are still retained among the people living there scarcely any doubt remains."

Considerable early evidence—circumstantial, at least—
that Madog reached American shores and established a settlement, is also supplied by England's great rival in exploration and colonization: Spain.

There was general belief in Spain that white men had inhabited the southeastern part of what is now the United
States prior to Columbus' voyage; this is proven by the
efforts she made to find these people. The Spanish Archives
in Seville show clearly that the Spanish government sent
out several expeditions to locate the *gente blanca* (white
people) in this area. After 1492, Spain based her claim to
America on the "right of discovery, exploration, and occupation," and it was necessary, in order to validate that
claim, to make very sure that the fair-skinned people no
longer lived there.

Thus, in 1557, Parda de Luna journeyed east from Mexico. He reached the Alabama River, following it and the
Coosa, as far as the present Childersburg, Alabama. He
found no white colonists.

Herbert Eugene Bolton, in his introduction to Arredondo's *Historical Proof of Spain's Title to Georgia* tells us that
"soldiers and sailors dispatched by Governor Salinas in 1624
scoured the [present] Georgia-Carolina interior for a hundred and fifty leagues, but they found no trace of the ru-
moured *gente blanca à cabello* [white people with hair, that
is, beards?]. Another party sent out by Salinas had like success. A little later, Pedro de Tores, ten sailors and sixty Indians travelled four months in the back country . . . of
[what is now] Georgia and Alabama and covered in 1628
two hundred leagues. They too failed . . ."

Not for lack of effort or determination did these Spanish expeditions to locate the pre-Columbian white settlers fail. According to the great Cherokee chief, Oconostota, the Welshmen had moved farther north, out along the Missouri River, long before the Spanish search for them even began. But the term used has been *gente blanca*, white people; not Welsh. Is there any indication the Spanish knew of Prince Madog? That it was Welshmen they were seeking?

In 1947, Bernard Quaritch, the London bookseller, auctioned a manuscript listed in his Catalogue No. 713 as follows:

> 222. HARO (Biud de) *Anatomie of Spayne*. Composed in the Castilian tonge bu Don-Biud de Haro. Anº 1598. Translated into Englishe by Harye Bedwood, gent. 1599.

The manuscript, purchased by Yale University, is an historical account of Spain and her monarchy, whose cruelty and tyranny the author stresses. On page 33 of this work is a long paragraph under the heading, "Presumcions to prove ye Spaniardes not to be ye first discoverers of the Yndes" wherein he cites Madog, son of a Prince of Wales, as the true discoverer. This would indicate that Madog's voyage was known to Biud de Haro's countrymen—or some of them, anyway.

Finally, Spain signed a treaty with England in 1670 agreeing that possession and occupation were sufficient proof of title. This was, of course, well after the Spanish expeditions cited above had failed to find the *gente blanca*. It is perhaps significant that following this treaty no more attempts to locate them were made.

Thus, it should be plain to reasonable people that an adventurous, sea-loving, handsome, easy-going man named Madog, a son of Owain, King of Gwynedd, lived—and sailed west—in the latter half of the twelfth century. We have seen *why* he left Gwynedd; let us now try to find out whence, under what conditions, and how far, he traveled.

 CHAPTER 2

A Prince Sails West

FIRST OF ALL, HOW did Prince Madog acquire the skill that allowed him to take a flimsy boat across the vast open ocean, daring its storms and swells and depths, in order to see if anything lay beyond the horizon? Brave his soul, indeed; but experience was as necessary as courage.

There is some slight evidence that Madog went to London as a young man, later sailing down the Thames, out around France and Spain into the Mediterranean. Supposedly he stayed in this area three years, trading from port to port—from Venice to the great cities of Phoenicia; from Orihuela to Mahdia, from Alexandria to Genoa—learning much all the while about navigation and astronomy. More certain it is that, growing up in Gwynedd, he spent much time as a youth in a coracle, the unique Welsh fisherman's boat—it holds only one man—on the rough waters of Caernarvon Bay and Menai Strait. In fact, there is an ancient Welsh poem in an unknown hand that describes Madog as "a skilled handler of the coracle, both on river and sea."

Later confirmation of these facts occurs in a prose account by one Roger Morris, dated March 13, 1582, where he asserts that "the son of Owain Gwynedd was a great sailor, much given to voyaging far afield," and that, to assist himself, he built "a ship without nails, but fastened with stag horns so that the sea would not swallow it." (Presumably, Madog did not want the weight that the great, heavy iron nails of the time would have added. Also, he may have had an extremely crude compass—a bit of lodestone floating on wooden sticks, such as the Vikings employed—and feared metal nails would distort its action.) In this ship, which he named *Gwennan Gorn*, Madog—continues Morris—"traversed the seas . . . and visited many foreign lands without fear or misadventure."

It would seem, then, that the Welsh prince's courage was supported by at least some practice in sailing familiar waters under adverse conditions.

Crossing the Atlantic Ocean was, of course, quite another matter. It has been argued that without the magnetic needle, not developed until the fourteenth century—and used by Columbus—a successful voyage would have been impossible; and, further, that a craft capable of such a feat did not yet exist. But we know the North Atlantic *had* been explored centuries before Madog. Eric the Red left Iceland in 982, returning three years later to report good fishing in the land later named Greenland. His son, Leif Ericsson, is believed to have landed on the northern coast of North America in 1002.

And, primitive as twelfth-century navigation was, it was up to the task. That there are two mighty ocean currents, one flowing westward from Europe, the other one back

again, was common knowledge by this time. The directions
of the prevailing winds were well known. The ancient
Phoenicians, Syrians, Greeks, and Romans, though never
venturing out of sight of land, traveled their waters by observation of the heavens; and long before Madog's era
northern seamen were sailing by the sun and the pole star.
The Druids, the high priests and medicine men of ancient
Wales, were no mean astronomers; and the Welsh language of the twelfth century reflected that fact in including
so early the words *seron, seronydd,* and *seronddiaeth,*
meaning in English star, astronomer, and astronomy; *not*
astrologer or astrology.

Thus, though luck and the sea rover's instinct may have
played some small part, Madog, by watching the sky and
making use of the Canaries current and North Equatorial
current, and favorable trade winds, could have been carried—in 1170—to the coast of what is now Florida and
Alabama.

In what? Unfortunately, no authentic drawings of the
ships of the period have come down to us. But from the
little that is known of twelfth-century British shipbuilding,
we can picture Madog's vessel, *Gwennan Gorn,* as being
single-masted, with a large, square sail. Buoyant and squat,
she had a straight, sturdy keel, in order to land more easily
at low tide. Probably there was a stern rudder, attached to
the sternpost by thongs. Obviously, she was slow-moving
and awkward to handle, but required only a small crew.

Could a little, frail craft such as this have sustained the
long journey across the storm-ravaged Atlantic? It could
indeed. Many such crossings have been made in recent
years just to prove this very point: that such voyages of

discovery, in the twelfth and even earlier centuries, were possible.

In 1952, a young French physician named Alain Louis Bombard traversed the Atlantic alone, in fifty-one days, on a little raft (fourteen by six feet) made of two metal cylinders lashed together. A built-in wooden stern held a slender six-foot mast with a small sail; one paddle, of a pair, served as a rudder.

Small as Dr. Bombard's raft was, the tiniest craft to cross the Atlantic, that we know of, was the *Nonoalca*, only twelve feet long. The little boat did it in sixty-five days, in 1966.

Finally, we know that in 1897, two men *rowed* from New York to the Scilly Islands, off the southwestern coast of England, in fifty-five days.

With his own records—if any were made—forever lost to us, we can only guess whether Madog sailed alone, except for his crew, on *Gwennan Gorn* or whether other ships and men joined him in his first Atlantic venture. We do know that by the fifteenth century, reports of the voyage had grown from one, or possibly two, ships to a fleet of thirteen, and from a company of twenty to over three hundred. Sir Thomas Herbert, a widely traveled scholar who wrote with unusual accuracy in his time, set down these large figures in his *Relation of Some Years Travaile*, issued in 1634; but the library containing the manuscripts he quotes as his source of information has long since been destroyed by fire.

Any undocumented story is exaggerated with the passage of time and frequent retelling, and it seems most unlikely there was such a large expedition. For one thing, that many ships departing at once—and for an unknown destination— would have attracted wide attention. So many bards and chroniclers would have noted the unusual event that multiple accounts, agreeing in detail, would surely survive. Then, there is the matter of financing such a great undertaking. Madog was a prince, true; but, as we have seen, because of all the dissension following—and even preceding —Owain's death, hardly an affluent one. Could he have paid for so many ships? And manned and provisioned them? And, just supposing he could have, what extraordinary charm did he possess to persuade that many men—doubtless more timid and fearful than he—to venture out into the deep, open ocean, knowing well they might never see beautiful Wales, or family, again?

Far more likely it is that a lone ship, the *Gwennan Gorn*, with a crew of about twenty, sailed quietly away that May morning eight centuries ago.

As to the provisions taken along, we can only assume them to be the usual things carried by other ships of the time on their shorter voyages: fresh water, of course; wine, dried meats, dried fish, coarse meal, cheese, and whatever else, that would not spoil, the small ship could hold to satisfy hearty appetites made even greater by hard work and salt sea air.

The port from which Madog set out is, like most other details, controversial. But we can at once state that it was *not*, as the name might suggest, and many have thought, Portmadoc. (Madoc is the modern Welsh spelling for Madog.) Both Portmadoc and nearby Tremadoc are named for the Welsh industrialist, William Alexander Madocks, who lived from 1773 to 1828. No map of Wales prior to 1800 shows either town.

James Howel in his *Epistolae Ho-Eloanae* (published in 1645-55) says the port was Milford Haven. But this was not in Gwynedd territory and, besides, we know that in 1170 it was being used by Henry II to assemble an expedition against Ireland. Thus, it is doubtful that Madog would have been able to use it.

Sir Thomas Herbert says Madog sailed from Abergwili. Again, this was not in Gwynedd. Even more important, the bridge the Romans built there still existed in Madog's day; it would have been very difficult, if not impossible, for a ship to sail out beneath it.

It seems more reasonable to believe that, strife-torn as it was, Madog, Prince of Gwynedd, would have outfitted his ship (or ships) and left from his homeland. Within it, sites from which one could have sailed even a very small vessel would have been limited to the estuary of the Dee, the river Clwyd, Abergele, Rhos-on-Sea, Conway, Bangor, the Menai Strait, Caernarvon, Nevin, Pwllheli or Abersoch. Did not Herbert write Abergele, and the printer simply misread his handwriting—perhaps none too clear—and printed Abergwili? Or, Herbert himself may have so misread his manuscript source.

But from whatever port, with courage stout Madog sailed westward, his destination unknown but for legend. The Druids had long claimed there was a "fair land to the West"; Taliesen, the great sixth-century bard, whose poems would doubtless have been well known to Prince Madog, spoke of a "magic country beyond the looking glass of the sea."

And about the time of Taliesen, St. Brandon of Ireland—
it is said—sailed the Atlantic for seven long years, touching
many unknown islands. Why did Madog sail west? From
all accounts he was a big, bluff, hearty man; perhaps he
would have given, in addition to the above reasons, the now
classic twentieth-century answer: because it was there.

Lacking records, we have no way of knowing how long
the voyage of discovery took. Herbert contents himself with
saying it was "long": "Anno 1170 he [Madog] left his coun-
trie, and after long saile and no less patience, blest with
some happy winds, at last descried land in the Gulph of
Mexico not farre from Florida." We now know that even
a small ship, carrying the minimum of sail—if "blest with
happy winds" and within the ocean current—could have
made about fourteen knots per hour. Thomas Stephens, a
Merthyr Tydfil chemist and distinguished Welsh scholar,
in a brilliant essay written in 1858, refers to Madog as
"sail[ing] for nine weeks on an open sea." How Stephens
arrived at this figure, no one seems to know; but it is a reasonable estimate.

His route would have been southward, at first, leaving
the coast of Wales on his port; past Ynys-yr-Hyrddod, the
Isles of the Blest; past the Azores; then gradually westward.
Where Madog made landfall we cannot know for certain,
but following the powerful ocean currents, as he was sure
to do, would bring him to the coast of southern Florida, described by a later explorer, Hernando de Soto, as "a land
full of bogs and poisonous fruits, barren and the very worst
country that is warmed by the sun." (At the time De Soto
wrote, "Florida" was a term used for all of America.) Surely
Madog would have sailed on, into the Gulf of Mexico,

searching for a suitable harbor. And what better spot than
Mobile Bay, a perfect natural landing place, surrounded
and protected by hills?

Presumably, Madog found the land good, left a few of
his company there, and returned to Gwynedd, where he
reported what he had seen, and then undertook a second
voyage to bring more colonists to the new country. Again,
to quote Herbert's account of Madog's initial trip: ". . . they
descried land . . . not farre from Florida, a land affording
health, aire, gold, good water and plenty of Nature's blessing, by which Prince Madoc was overjoyed and had reason
to account his happy estate, superiour to that his brothers
strive for, so eagerly emulating with ambitious hate and
bloud [blood] each other even for a little Territory, incom-
parable to that good destiny allotted him, being a vast and
weal Kingdome, obtained in some part without opposition,
and able to satiate the most covetous." In this "happy
estate," continues Herbert, Madog "planted, fortified some
advantagious places . . . and returned home after some bad
windes, guided by supremme providence and the benefit the
Pole-Starre gave him in the night.

"When he had landed and had accounted his happy and
miraculous voyage, told the hopes of succeeding Conquests,
and other motives of persuasion and admiration, these and
the words of Madoc himselfe drew so many willing minds
and purses to a returne, that he attempted it with ten good
Barques, loaded with all necessary provisions . . ."

Herbert makes no reference to the sailing point of the
second expedition; but Meiron, an eighteenth-century poet
who interested himself in the matter, says it was the Isle of

Lundy: "The country [Gwynedd] became embroiled in civil war. Influenced by disgust, Madoc, who is represented as of a very mild disposition, resolved upon the matchless enterprise of exploring the ocean westwards, in search of more tranquil scenes. The event was, according to various documents, the discovering of a new world, from which he effected his return to inform his country of his good fortune. The consequence of which was the fitting out of a second expedition, and Madoc, with his brother Riryd, Lord of Clochran in Ireland, prevailed upon so many to accompany them as to fill seven ships and, sailing from the Isle of Lundy, they took an eternal leave of Wales." Others, though, say the fleet departed from a small port near the present Holyhead on the Isle of Anglesey.

Surely we can assume that Madog followed the same route on this second voyage as on the first. Carried along by the same currents, he once more came near the Gulf of Mexico. Yet it is highly improbable that he landed at the very same place, or even in the same region. Thus, this time Madog might have been borne north, by the Gulf Stream, along the eastern coast of what it now Florida; or maybe to the Bahamas or other Caribbean islands; or even to the coast of Mexico. Perhaps he reached the island of Guadeloupe; at any rate, Antonio de Herrera, a Spanish historian, asserts that Columbus came upon the wreckage of some ships at Guadeloupe, and could not otherwise account for them. (Incidentally, Peter Martyr of Anghiera, an Italian geographer and historian, who was frequently invited to the Spanish court by Ferdinand V and presumably was present when Columbus returned from his epic voyage, tells

us in his *De Orbe Decades Octo* (1530) that Columbus was
well aware of Madog's earlier voyages. As proof, Martyr
says that Columbus had written on one of his maps, somewhere in the vicinity of the West Indies, *Questo he mar de
Cambrio*—these are Welsh waters.)

As usual, opinion differs as to the number of ships that
sailed on the second, colonizing expedition. Some say ten;
others seven; still others, fewer. And the number of men—
women were needed too—ranges from 120 up to three hundred. But however many, evidently Madog, returning to
Gwynedd in 1171, had little trouble convincing people he
had discovered a new land, free from the strife he detested,
where one could live out his life in peace.

Little is known—or even speculated—concerning what
happened to the persons Madog left in the new country on
his first trip. About the only statement is one by—again—
Sir Thomas Herbert, relating how Madog, upon his return
voyage to America, "found many of his Britaines dead,
caused by the Natives' villainy, or alternation of the clime,
which notwithstanding, he digested patiently, and . . . bet-
tered the first intention, living with content, and dying in no
less distance from Heaven than when at home, unhappiest
in this that their own Nation forgot them quite either judg-
ing them lost, because never after hearing from them, or
because their own Beings were turned topsie turvy." (As
stated earlier, Herbert believed up to three hundred men
and thirteen ships sailed on the first voyage.)

We are brought now to the ultimate fate of Madog. So
far as can be discovered in the records that have come down
to us, after making landfall in the New World a second time
—or failing to do so—Madog is never mentioned again.

It is plain from the above quotation that Herbert believed
Madog to have ended his earthly days in the new land he discovered. Many investigators have agreed. James Howel,
cited earlier, was one, asserting that Madog died in the
West Indies, and quoting a set of verses in medieval Welsh
found on his tomb in one of the islands, where it had lain
"nere upon 600 yeares since." Roughly translated into English prose the epitaph Howel refers to reads: "Weary of a
life of bloodshed and rapine in Gwynedd, I sailed with ten
ships and three hundred men towards a country much re-
cited in the annals of our Druids; a distant world which lay
in the west. After thirteen weeks, battered, famished and
disheartened, we reached it at last. There for twice thirty
years I and my people lived in happiness and peace, possessing wealth not dreamed of in hungry Wales." However,
archaeologists have yet to uncover any such tomb.

Still other historians are certain that Madog and his colonists never reached land, but perished at sea. What seems
at first glance to be confirmation of this fact was brought
forth several years ago by the late Reverend E. F. Synnott
of Iden, in Kent, England. One day, at an auction in Sussex,
he bought a collection of old books. Among them he found
some very old, moldy manuscripts. Many of them were torn
and even partially charred, as if they had been hastily
rescued from a fire. Mr. Synnott, patiently fitting the pieces
together, found he had some port records for the twelfth
and thirteenth centuries. Partly in Latin and partly in
broken English, they seemed to be a simple listing of ships
lost, or unaccounted for, from the various ports of England
and Wales.

Among the entries was this one:

Aber-Kerrick-Guignon:
non sunt
Guignon Gorn, Madauc
Pedr Sant, Riryd, filius
Oueni Gueneti
an. 1171.

This is interesting, indeed, but raises several questions. First, where is Aber-Kerrick-Guignon? No place so named appears on any map of the period. Mr. Synnott's own theory, and a reasonable one, was that this ancient port may have, in time, become known by a shortened form, Aber Kerrick, or Aberkerry, and then finally, Abergele.

According to this old record, Madog's brother Riryd accompanied him in a second ship. If so, why did Edwall and Einion, also exiled by Dafydd, not go along—each perhaps in command of his own ship? Or did they do so, as Herbert states, but only Madog and Riryd are mentioned in the port record?

And why is only Riryd identified as the son of Owain of Gwynedd? Possibly this reflects Madog's illegitimacy; or perhaps Riryd, as Lord of Clochran, was known to possess great estates, whereas Madog—as we have seen—was ever something of a nomad, possessing no lands. We just don't know.

Also, on the document no mark appears opposite the name of Madog's ship, the *Gwennan Gorn* (given a French spelling in the manuscript); but by that of the *Pedr Sant* (*Saint Peter*) there is the sign of the cross and a short, illegible word. Does the sign of the cross indicate sure knowledge that Riryd's ship was sunk? Whereas Madog's was never heard from again, and therefore just presumed to be lost?

And if there were seven to ten ships, why are the others not mentioned?

Finally, the year is given as 1171. This is the year Madog returned to Gwynedd from his first voyage—there seem to be enough witnesses to that fact to make it all but unquestionable. And it seems unlikely he would have been able to procure ships, outfit them, enlist colonists, and depart all in the same half year, for only about that portion would be fit sailing weather on the North Atlantic.

Whatever really happened in that far-off, long ago time, one thing at least appears certain: Madog never returned to live in Gwynedd. One hopes he found the peaceful home he longed for, on American soil. Or—if it had to be—an eternal resting place beneath the sea he loved so well, feared so little, and traveled so far.

But let us now examine the evidence for a flourishing Welsh colony, planted by Madog, more than three hundred years before Columbus led his three ships into "Welsh waters."

CHAPTER 3

Welsh Indians?

IF, AS THERE IS GOOD reason for believing, Madog was able to land his colonists somewhere on the North American shore, and they were not exterminated by "the Natives' villainy, or alternation of the clime," it is obvious that in time the colonists themselves, their children, and their descendants would marry some of those "Natives." And the issue of such marriages would be: light-skinned Indians speaking the Welsh language. It is the reports—continuing over two centuries—of just such "Welsh Indians" that should now be considered.

The first account comes from David Ingram, of Barking, in Essex, England. Ingram was one of nearly a hundred men put ashore "about 100 leagues west and by north from the Cape of Florida" in 1568, by Sir John Hawkins. (In a fierce encounter with the Spaniards, Sir John had lost a ship, and could not accommodate all his men in the two that remained to him.) "About 12 months" later, Ingram and two companions reached "the river called Gorinda [the St. John River in New Brunswick, Canada] 60 leagues west of Cape Britton." From there, they were taken by a French ship back to England.

At home, Ingram wrote his *Relation* of his adventure. In it, he states that he met with Indians who used Welsh terms for various objects, "and other Welsh words, a matter worth the noting." Very much so! Ingram seems to have been both a careful and keen observer. Of Indian corn he wrote: "ear as big as man's wrist, grain like a flat pease, maketh good bread and white." His statement that he saw elephants on his journey long drew smiles from his readers, if not laughter; but it has been confirmed by the fairly recent finding of a mastodon skeleton under circumstances that indicate it lived in America as late as the end of the sixteenth century. Thus, Ingram's remarks about Welsh-speaking Indians are not to be shrugged off.

But while the first mention of Welsh Indians in America came, naturally enough, from the early English and Spanish explorers, they knew little of the Welsh tongue or customs; and it was not until the Welsh themselves began to emigrate in numbers that detailed reports of such a tribe were made.

One of the earliest such accounts is contained in a letter, written March 10, 1686, by the Reverend Morgan Jones, then rector of the Welsh Presbyterian Church of Newtown, on Long Island. The letter was sent to Dr. Thomas Lloyd, the noted Welsh Quaker leader of Philadelphia. In it Jones relates that twenty years before, in the year 1666, he was chaplain to Major General Richard Bennett, former governor of Virginia, when an expedition, by ship, to South Carolina was undertaken. Upon arrival, Morgan Jones was dispatched inland to a place named Oyster Point, where he was to serve as minister to a newly formed colony. He remained there eight months, suffering great hardship. Then, "starved for provisions," he decided to leave and return overland, on foot, to Virginia.

"I and five more traveled through the wilderness till we came to Tuscarora Country," he wrote. "There the Tuscora [sic] Indians took us prisoners. . . . That night they took us to their town and shut us close to our no small dread.

"The next day they entered into consultation about us, which after it was over the interpreter told us that we must prepare to die the next morning. Thereupon, being much dejected, and speaking to this effect in British [that is, Welsh] tongue: 'Have I escaped so many dangers and must I now be knocked on the head like a dog?' Presently an Indian came to me which afterwards appeared to be a War Captain belonging to the Sachem of the Doegs, whose origin I find is from the old British, and took me and told me in the British tongue that I should not die, and thereupon went to the Emperor and agreed for my ransom.

"They then welcomed me to their town where they entertained us for four months during which time I had the opportunity of conversing with them familiarly, and did preach to them three times a week in the same language and they would confer with me about anything that was difficult therein; and at our departure they supplied us with what was necessary to our support and well being.

"This is a brief recital of my travels among the Doeg Indians. They are settled on the Pontiago River, not far from Camp Atros. I am ready to conduct any Welshman, or others, to the country."

One can't help wondering why Jones waited so many years to write about his experience; and why—in doing so—

he gave such a short account of the matter, with no verification from his five comrades, whose names are not even given. And there is no evidence that his revelation was followed by any expedition to the Tuscarora region to investigate.

Some authorities have questioned the truthfulness of Morgan Jones' account, saying that no one—before or since —has had any knowledge of a tribe of Indians named the Doegs. Yet in 1673, Giovanni Paolo Marana, an Italian-born Turkish spy, who lived in Paris for forty-five years without being detected, published an eight-volume work, *Letters Writ by a Turkish Spy*. In it, he refers to the Doegs as descended from the Welsh and even mentions the Sachem! True, Marana's book was issued several years after Jones' adventure, but thirteen years before he, Jones, wrote his letter to Dr. Lloyd. Presumably then, Marana could have known nothing of Morgan Jones' experience. And in late years, a few historians have suggested that the Doegs might have been a small sect of the powerful Delaware tribe.

During the remainder of the seventeenth—and throughout the eighteenth—century, reports of Welsh-speaking Indians multiplied.

Sometime between 1660 and 1665, a Welsh sailor from Brecon whose last name was Stedman was shipwrecked on the Atlantic and washed ashore somewhere between Florida and Virginia—a very big area, but he does not identify the place more closely. Stedman was discovered by friendly Indians who, he said, spoke a language so similar to his own that he understood them at once. When he replied—in Welsh—to their questions, they understood him and were amazed. They then "supplied him with the best things they had. They told [him] that their ancestors had come from a country named Gwynedd in Prydain Fawr" [Great Britain], though this latter name did not come into general usage until at least 1603. And again, the story was not printed until many, many years later, after Charles Lloyd, to whom Stedman related his adventure, wrote about it in a letter which the Reverend Nicholas Owen came upon and published in his *British Remains* in 1777, more than a century after Stedman's encounter.

Next, a Mr. Binion—his first name is unknown—who had traded among the Indians for over thirty years, reported that about 1750 he and a few companions pushed west of the Mississippi River. To their amazement, they found a tribe of Indians who spoke Welsh. "They lived in stone-built villages, and were better clothed than the other tribes. There were ruined buildings; one among them appeared very like an old Welsh castle, another like a ruined church." When Mr. Binion told the Indians he had come to America from Wales, they said, "It was from thence that our ancestors came, but we do not know in what part of the world Wales is."

In 1753, a Colonel George Chrochan wrote a letter to Governor Dinwiddie of Virginia. In it he mentioned that three young French priests had just returned from a missionary trip among the Indians, and brought back with them a Welsh Bible which the Indians had in their possession! Something is very wrong here. If there was such a book, it would have to have been a psalter, missal, or some other ancient manuscript. Madog and his colonists could hardly have carried Welsh Bibles into America centuries before it was translated into that language, let alone printed.

About 1764, or somewhat later, Captain Isaac Stewart, a dashing young officer in the Provincial Cavalry of South Carolina, was taken prisoner by Indians while he was on a mission about fifty miles west of Fort Pitt. He and his companions were led westward by their captors to the banks of the Wabash River. There, unfortunately, his comrades were killed under "circumstances of horrid barbarity," and Stewart himself was doomed. However, the gallant captain seems to have caught the eye of an Indian maiden, who ransomed him with a horse. He was kept prisoner, however —we hear nothing more of the maiden—until a Spaniard, sent out from Mexico on an exploratory expedition, visited the Indians and asked the chief to release Captain Stewart and a Welshman, John David, who had somehow escaped execution. The chief agreed, and Stewart and David accompanied the unnamed Spaniard across the Mississippi River near the Red River, then traveled north for seven hundred miles.

In an article in the *Public Advertiser*, a Louisville, Kentucky, newspaper, for October 8, 1785, Captain Stewart describes what happened next: ". . . we came to a nation of Indians, remarkably white and whose hair was a reddish colour, at least mostly so. The day after our arrival the Welshman [John David] informed me that he was determined to remain with them, giving as a reason that he understood their language, it being very little different from the Welsh.

"My curiosity was excited very much by this information, and I went with my companion to the chief men of the town, who informed him (in a language that I had no knowledge of, and which had no affinity to that of any other

Indian tongues that I ever heard) that their forefathers in this nation came from a foreign country, and landed on the east side of the Mississippi, describing particularly the country called Florida, and that on the Spaniards taking possession of Mexico, they fled to their then abode.

"And, as a proof of what he had advanced, he brought forth rolls of parchment, which were carefully tied up in otter skins, on which were large characters written with blue ink. The characters I did not understand, and the Welshman, being unacquainted with letters, [that is, unable to read] I was not able to know the meaning of the writing. They are a bold, hardy, and intrepid people, very warlike, and the women beautiful, when compared with the other Indians." They were, Stewart said, "high-browed, [with] blueish eyes and perfect lips." Unfortunately, he does not identify this remarkable tribe by name.

Morgan Lewis, famed general of the Revolutionary War and later governor of New York, claimed that his father, a signer of the Declaration of Independence, had good reason to know there were Welsh-speaking Indians in eastern America.

It seems that Francis Lewis, son of a clergyman, left Llandaff, Wales, when he was twenty-one and established himself as a merchant in New York. He took part in the French and Indian War, was captured by Montcalm in 1757, and taken—along with other prisoners—to Canada. Later he was released; but after the fall of Oswego, in New York, he was taken by Indians near Albany. At that time, said his son, Francis Lewis was tied to a stake to be burned alive, when he began speaking to his captors in his native

Francis Lewis, painted by A. Rosenthal

Welsh tongue. They understood him, and promptly released him.

This is not too convincing. Since Francis Lewis left no report of the incident, it is suspected that the story grew and was distorted with the years. Why should he have addressed the Indians in Welsh instead of English? Also, the site of the supposed incident is far from any reputed to be a home of the Welsh Indians. Still . . .

A Captain Abraham Chaplain, of Kentucky, "whose veracity may be entirely depended upon" stated that between 1770 and 1775, when he was stationed at a garrison in Kaskaskia, he met with some Indians who spoke Welsh. These Indians talked with two men from Wales under

Chaplain's command, and each group understood the other instantly.

Chaplain's account would appear to be corroborated by Benjamin Sutton. In 1775 or 1776 a missionary from New York, Charles Beatty, went about four hundred miles south of his home. There, he tells us, he met several men who had lived among Indians during their younger days. One of these was Benjamin Sutton, who had spent many years among various Indian nations and spoke freely of his experiences. He related that when he was among the Choctaws, considerably north of New Orleans, he came across a tribe that was "not so tawny as . . . other Indians . . . and spoke Welsh." How Sutton, non-Welsh, recognized the language is not explained. He did add, however, that he had overheard one of the Indians speaking in Welsh with one Captain Lewis, who was their prisoner. Francis Lewis, cited above, comes immediately to mind; but that incident occurred in eastern New York, not west of the Mississippi River and "a great distance above New Orleans."

We come now to the story of Maurice Griffith, which somewhat parallels that of Morgan Jones. Griffith left Wales when he was but sixteen, coming to Virginia. In 1764 he was captured by a band of Shawnees somewhere near the headwaters of the Roanoke River. They were friendly and he stayed with them some three or four years. Then five of the young braves were sent west on a hunting and exploring expedition—specifically, to find the source of the Missouri River. They took Griffith with them.

In the Rockies, Griffith and the five Shawnees came upon three "white men in Indian dress" whom they accompanied several days, until they reached an entire village of such light-skinned Indians. The account of what ensued was later published by Harry Toulmin, Secretary of State for Kentucky, in *The Palladium*, another Frankfort, Kentucky, newspaper:

"After proceeding with them four or five days' journey they came to the village of these white men, where they found the whole nation of the same colour, all having the European complexion . . . A council lasted three days and Griffith was present; he had not admitted that he knew their language. It was finally decided that the six strangers should be put to death, and Griffith thought the time had arrived for him to speak. He addressed the council in the Welsh language, said they had not been sent by any warlike nation and they were actuated by curiosity and had no hostile intentions; that they merely wished to trace the Missouri to its source and they would return to their country satisfied with the discovery they had made without any wish to disturb the repose of their new acquaintances.

"Astonishment glowed in the countenances not only of the council, but of his [Griffith's] Shawnee companions who clearly saw that he was understood. Confidence was given to his declarations. The King advanced and gave him his hand and from that moment they were treated with the utmost friendship. Griffith and his five Shawnee companions remained with the nation eight months. As to the history of these people Griffith could learn nothing satisfactory. All they knew was that their ancestors had come up the river from a very distant country. They had intermixed with no other people by marriage and there was not a dark-skinned man in the nation."

Griffith and the five braves went back east to the Shawnee encampment after being away for two and a half years. Griffith eventually returned to Virginia, and there are no more reports of him, though in May of 1805 his adventure received some confirmation from a Major Amos Stoddard, who wrote *Sketches, Historical and Descriptive, of Louisiana.* While in northern Louisiana, Stoddard met a Frenchman who had long been employed by English traders. His usual station was a trading post on the Assiniboine River, just a few days' journey from the Mandan settlement on the Missouri. The Frenchman, it developed, had also explored this river—the Missouri—to its source, and he told Stoddard "that there was a numerous and singular nation of Indians [there] who were not in the least tawny, but rather of a yellowish complexion; that they wear their beards and that great numbers of them had red hair on their heads."

Finally, for sheer drama, nothing quite matches the account of Lt. Joseph Roberts, a Welshman who, in 1801, encountered a face-painted, Welsh-speaking Indian chief in the dining room of a Washington, D. C., hotel. This incident was reported in the aforementioned *Public Advertiser* for May 15, 1819, eighteen years after it occurred; though an account of it did appear in Wales, in *Y Greal Neu Eurgrawn,* much earlier—in 1805.

After the surprise of finding that the Indian chief knew and spoke Welsh, Lieutenant Roberts continued to question him.

"I asked him if he would like to go to England and Wales; he replied that he had not the least inclination to leave his native country and that he would sooner live in a wigwam than a palace. He had ornamented his naked arms with bracelets and on his head were ostrich feathers.

"I was greatly astonished and greatly amazed when I heard such a man who painted his face yellowish-red and of such an appearance speaking the ancient British language as fluently as if he had been born and brought up in the vicinity of Snowdon. His head was shaved except around the crown and there the hair was very long and plaited, and it was on the crown of his head he had placed the ostrich feathers . . . to ornament himself.

"The situation of these Indians is about eight hundred miles southwest of Philadelphia, according to his statement, and they are called the Asguawa, or Asguaw nation.

"The chief courted my society astonishingly, seeing that we were descended from the same people. He used to call upon me almost every day and take me to the woods to show me the virtues of the various herbs which grew there, for neither he nor his people were acquainted with compounded medicine."

These have been but a few of the many reports current from 1686 through 1820 concerning the existence of a tribe, or tribes, of Welsh-speaking Indians in America.

But of the many such accounts, it was the Morgan Jones story that received the most publicity, on both sides of the Atlantic, and had the greatest repercussions. It was rewritten by Theophilus Evans under the title *The Crown of England's Title to America Prior to That of Spain,* and was published in the *Gentleman's Magazine* in 1740. That article was reprinted in Rovington's *New York Gazette* later that same year, in Nicholas Owen's *British Remains* in 1777, and in various other journals down to the early nineteenth century. What effect it had, we shall see.

CHAPTER 4

Plans to Investigate

THEOPHILUS EVANS'
article concerning Morgan Jones' terrifying encounter was,
above all else, timely. As we have noted, it was first printed
in 1740, a year when England was again at war with Spain
(the War of Jenkins' Ear) and was read eagerly. To think
that Britain should have a claim to America predating that
of her archrival and enemy, Spain! All that was lacking was
positive, documented proof that such light-skinned, Welsh-
speaking Indians existed.

Thus it was inevitable that, eventually, someone—from
Wales, of course, so he would know the language—would
be sent to America on an official search for such Indians.

But the British are seldom in a hurry, and things moved
very slowly.

In 1771, a sizable group of Welshmen living and working in London formed a social and literary Society, called
the Gweneddigion. The club met the first Monday of each
month. Since among its members were several outstanding
Welsh intellectuals, it became quite an influential group;

especially as its formation coincided with a quickened interest on the part of English scholars in all things Welsh, particularly old Celtic legends. Because of the role the Society played in the search for the Welsh Indians, we should take a brief look at three or four of its leading men.

Owen Jones, a wealthy furrier, was its chief patron. David Samwell, a former surgeon in the Royal Navy who had gone with Captain Cook on his voyages and saw him murdered by natives in the Hawaiian Islands, was very active in Gweneddigion affairs. He was also a minor poet. William Owen-Pughe, the Welsh lexicographer, compiler of the monumental *Dictionary of the Welsh Language*, had—with one exception—the widest reputation of any member.

That exception was Edward Williams, better known by his bardic name of Iolo Morganwg, whose intense interest in Prince Madog and his discovery of America was, unfortunately, to exceed his truthfulness, and make him forever a figure of shame in the annals of Welsh literature. While editing some genuine medieval Welsh manuscripts for publication, the *Myvyrian Archiaology*, he inserted among them his own poetic version of the Madog story. Owen Jones and William Owen-Pughe were co-editors; but the furrier, though deeply interested in Welsh antiquities, lacked the education to detect a pure fabrication, and Owen-Pughe's credulity was almost as great as his energy. When the volume appeared in 1801, it was accepted as authentic; but before very long the portion treating of Madog was proved a forgery. Iolo was declared a fraud and forced to retire in disgrace from the ranks of Welsh scholarship.

But in 1791 Iolo Morganwg was still a brilliant literary figure; a self-educated stonemason who had made himself

the authority on ancient literary history and the early Welsh
bards. His forging of old manuscripts lay ten years in the
future; and his deep, genuine interest in the reports of
Welsh Indians in America inspired other members of the
Gweneddigion Society.

In this year, 1791, a Dr. John Williams of Sydenham, who
had studied the matter for over thirty years, issued a tract
entitled *An Enquiry into the Truth of the Tradition Concerning the Discovery of America by Prince Madog ab
Owen Gwenedd about the Year 1170.* It reviewed all that
was known to date on the subject, and greatly intensified
the interest aroused years earlier by Theophilus Evans'
article.

The ink was little more than dry on Dr. Williams' pam-
phlet when a mysterious, colorful visitor from America
arrived in London. This was one William Augustus Bowles,
who referred to himself as "King," "Chief," or "General,"
according to his mood of the moment; though at the time of
his appearance in London, he actually was on official Indian
business and rightfully held the imposing title of Director
General of the Creek Nation.

Certainly a charlatan, liar, and adventurer, he was at the
same time a man to be reckoned with. He either had been
—or still was—an artist, actor, diplomat, navigator, musi-
cian, soldier, cook, hunter, linguist, lawyer, chemist—and
Indian chief. Born on the Maryland frontier in 1763, of
comfortable English parentage, he had—as Ensign Bowles,
aged sixteen—deserted the Maryland Loyalists during prep-
arations for a Franco-Spanish engagement near Pensacola.
Far from home and desperate, he attached himself to a
party of Creek Indians, little knowing that he was to spend
nearly all the remaining years of his life with them—this

Iolo Morganwg (Edward Williams), who inspired the expedition by John Evans

Another portrait of Iolo Morganwg, from an etching by Robert Cruikshank

by choice, as well as through two successive marriages to
Creek women.

In the elegant, formal London of 1791, William Bowles
excited stares and whispers wherever he went. Occasionally
he was merely picturesque, with his knee-length hunting
jacket and buckskin leggings; but most of the time he was
resplendent in a brilliant cloth turban, intricately wound
and sporting a waving ostrich plume, a heavy, half-moon
shaped silver gorget around his neck, and regular shirt and
breeches. At his side swung always a ceremonial silver
tomahawk, indicating his war chief status.

Naturally, such a handsome, flamboyant figure, though
ever a bit vague as to his reasons for being in London, was
welcomed into the highest English society. The Prince of
Wales and the Duke of Gloucester, of the royal family, entertained him; so did Lord George Townshend and other
members of the nobility.

Bowles was equally popular in the taverns. A fine con-
versationalist, he would—in return for plenty of hard liquor
—entertain clients by the hour with highly colored, greatly
exaggerated tales of his life and adventures on the American frontier.

Of course it wasn't long until the Gweneddigion Society
heard about the newcomer in its midst. Here was a chance
to find out at firsthand about the Welsh Indians. After all,
the gaudily dressed Bowles had lived all his life among
Indians, hadn't he? Surely, he would know if there really
was a fair-complexioned, Welsh-speaking tribe. Accord-
ingly, Samwell and Owen-Pughe were commissioned by the
Society to call upon "General" Bowles, question him closely,
and report back to the membership.

William Augustus Bowles
From an engraving of Thomas Hardy's portrait

Bowles did not disappoint his visitors. Indeed, he informed the two scholars that the "legend" was quite true;
there were white, Welsh-speaking Indians in America. But
how could he be so sure, asked Owen-Pughe and Samwell.
Though a linguist of sorts, Bowles admitted to the merest
smattering of Welsh. But that objection was easy for the
Director General to answer.

"A Welshman was with me at home for some time,"
Bowles explained; "he had been a prisoner among the Spaniards and worked in the mines of Mexico. By some means

he contrived to escape, got into the wilds and made his way
across the continent, and eventually found himself with a
people with whom he could converse and stayed there some
time." Bowles went on to identify the particular tribe as
the Padoucas. Immediately Owen-Pughe, the dictionary
maker, felt certain this name was but the slight, natural
corruption of *Madogwys* (pronounced Măd·ŏg·ōō′ĭs) or,
"the people of Madog."

Filled with enthusiasm, the two Welshmen hastened to
tell the Gweneddigion men of their findings; and at that
precise moment was born the Society's determination to
dispatch a mission to America to find the Welsh Indians. A
supplement to Dr. Williams' book, entitled—appropriately
enough—*Further Observations on the Discovery of America
by Prince Madog ab Owen Gwenedd about the Year 1170,*
provided still more inspiration for the venture. Iolo Morganwg himself would lead the expedition. And at successive
meetings, the members debated the matter endlessly, pored
over maps of America in an attempt to discover the home
territory of the Padoucas, and studied ways of raising the
necessary money.

But it is difficult for a group of diverse personalities to
maintain feverish interest in any project for long. Soon Iolo
—and others—began to have second thoughts. Fierce argument arose. David Samwell wrote a poem describing these
rather comic, though sincere, disputes. Next, Iolo withdrew;
he would not go on "the Padouca hunt." This decision, however, seems not to have resulted from loss of interest. All his
life, Iolo had yearned to go to America; his three brothers
had long since left Wales to live in the West Indies. But Iolo
was now forty-six years old, with a sizable family to sup-

port, and more reputation than income. He simply could not afford to go. With his defection, Gweneddigion concern with the project dwindled, though it did not die.

Meanwhile, during these many months, interest in locating the Welsh Indians had developed in Wales itself. About this time, William Jones of Llangadfan, a radical—for that era—poet, and defender of the oppressed Welsh peasantry, hiked the country over, despite his sixty-odd years, shouting against the greedy landlords and recommending emigration to America. One night in particular—July 13, 1791—speaking near Llanrwst, he warmed to his theme and became very eloquent and persuasive. Over there, promised Jones, settlement near their kinsmen—the Welsh Indians—would be sure to provide trade. Living conditions would be vastly improved. There would be enough of everything for all. And in the audience that night, spellbound, sat a young man who . . .

But the strange saga of John Evans deserves its own chapter.

CHAPTER 5

The Strange Saga
of John Evans

ON THE NIGHT OF January 13, 1804, President Thomas Jefferson, of Welsh ancestry and able to speak the ancient language, sat late at his desk writing a letter to his former secretary, also a Welsh-American. This was Meriwether Lewis, soon to set out, with William Clark, on an expedition to learn whether or not a water route connected the Mississippi River with the Pacific Ocean. Jefferson sent with his letter a map of the upper Missouri River valley. Concerning this enclosure, the President wrote, "I now enclose you a map of the Missouri as far as the Mandans, 12 or 1500 miles I presume above its mouth; it is said to be very accurate having been done by a Mr. John Evans by order of the Spanish government."

Jefferson would have known that Evans is a Welsh surname; but obviously he knew nothing of the short, troubled life of the man who had drawn the map—a map so accurate

that Lewis and Clark made only the most minor correc-
tions on it.

John Thomas Evans, whose father and older brother were
Welsh Methodist preachers in the Caernarvon district of
North Wales, was born in the long, straggling village of
Waunfawr in 1770. His education was that usual to a boy
of the era and country—with one exception. The village
schoolmaster was Dafydd Ddu Eryri (David Thomas) a
well-known poet. It would appear that Thomas had been
much impressed with the lad, for upon discovering his interest in the Welsh Indians of America—this interest aroused
by the fiery William Jones' exhortation to his younger countrymen to emigrate—Thomas wrote to friends in the Gweneddigion Society in London, proposing young Evans as the
ideal companion for Iolo Morganwg in the forthcoming
search for the Welsh-speaking Indians.

Evans was invited to London. There, he talked frequently
with "General" Bowles, mining everything that vivid figure
knew about the matter. And when Iolo, immediately attracted to Evans, abandoned his plans for the long journey,
he proposed that the eager young man—John Evans was
but twenty-one—go in his stead, and alone.

So it was that in September of 1792, with a small sum of
money—presumably supplied in large part by Owen Jones,
the well-to-do Thames Street furrier—and the blessing of
the Gweneddigion Society, John Evans, from on board ship,
watched the green hills of Wales recede. He was never to
see them again.

Landing in Baltimore on October 10, he set out immediately, on foot, for the Welsh settlements of Pennsylvania.

He had letters of introduction to several distinguished citi-
zens there, and was very warmly received by them. The
two most influential leaders of the Welsh colony were William Pritchard, a bookseller in Philadelphia, and Dr. Samuel
Jones, pastor—for fifty-one years—at nearby Pennepek and
founder of Rhode Island College, later Brown University.
Yet, when Evans explained his quest, each of these men
urged him not to penetrate Indian territory; it was much
too dangerous, they said. But Evans was young, confident,
energetic—and he had never met an Indian.

By now, though, he realized he would need more money
than the Society had been able to provide. Then too, winter was coming on. He returned to Baltimore and found
himself a job as bookkeeper and general clerk in the office
of two merchants. Evidently he did his work well, for his
employers offered to set him up in a business if he would
stay in the area.

But John Evans was determined to carry out his mission,
come spring. And during the few months in Baltimore,
apart from his clerkship, he was not idle. Owen-Pughe and
the Gweneddigíon men, relying heavily on "General"
Bowles' tales, were sure the Padoucas were the descendants
of Madog; but from his subsequent reading and listening,
Evans was not so certain. He was inclined to think it was
the Mandan tribe he sought. In either case, he would find
the Welsh Indians far up the Missouri River. Evans got
maps and, during the long winter evenings, pondered his
route. He could, after revisiting the Welsh colony in Pennsylvania, travel north into Canada and join a fur-trading
expedition to the Missouri; or he could go southwest, into
Spanish territory, and sail up the river. After much study,

The Reverend Dr. Samuel Jones

Thomas Jefferson, painted by James Sharples, Sr.

he chose the latter. Had he but taken the northern way . . .

Thus, in March of 1793, Evans gathered together his few belongings, his maps and his savings, and left for Philadelphia. Once more, he was warned by the Welshmen there, especially Pritchard and Dr. Jones, against entering Indian lands. These repeated admonitions, plus the fact that neither of these men had collected a cent toward his expenses, seem to have soured Evans on his fellow countrymen in America. If so, this may explain, in part anyway, the strangest thing he ever did—*if* indeed he did it—five years later.

Nettled, but eager to go on with his quest, young Evans pushed into the interior of Pennsylvania, across the Susquehanna River, over the Allegheny Mountains, to Fort Pitt. There, he took a flatboat seven hundred miles down the Ohio River to its junction with the Mississippi. A river boat carried him two hundred more miles up that river and deposited him—several weeks after leaving Baltimore—in St. Louis, where the Missouri River enters the Mississippi.

He could not have arrived at a more inopportune time. St. Louis was the hub of a four-power political struggle: the United States of America, so newly born as a nation, was anxious to expand westward. Her explorers had reached the great Mississippi, and already had posts at Cahokia and Kaskaskia, just across the river from St. Louis. Britain, in Canada, had—as early as 1670—formed the Hudson's Bay Company to trade furs with the Indians, and constantly threatened to push southward. France, in eastern Canada— along the St. Lawrence and around the Great Lakes—had formed a loose association called the North West Company, and the rivalry between it and the British Hudson's Bay

Company was bitter and intense. And the infiltration of both these companies into the upper reaches of the Mississippi and Missouri Rivers was most disturbing to Spain, the fourth power, who—as a result of the Seven Years War— now owned all land west of the Mississippi. The center of government for this vast, largely unexplored empire was St. Louis, in 1793 a village of about a thousand white people, mostly French-speaking, and nearly three hundred Negro slaves.

To administer this enormous possession came, as Governor, Don François Louis Hector, Baron de Carondelet de Noyelles, Seigneur d'Haine Saint Pierre, member of a famed Burgundian family that had entered the service of Spain. He arrived in New Orleans in January of 1792. At the same time, Don Zenon Trudeau, an able and industrious man, was appointed Lieutenant-Governor in St. Louis.

Very shortly after Trudeau took office, and at his instigation, there was formed the Missouri Company, or Compaña Explorada; its purpose to discover a route across the Rocky Mountains that would link the Mississippi Valley with the Spanish settlements in California. It was charged with building forts all along the route, and was granted exclusive trading rights on the upper Missouri. This activity—encouraged by the Governor, Carondelet, despite the fact that the Company consisted solely of merchants whose motive was the exploitation of the Indians for private gain—would require the greatest secrecy, of course. The other three powers—England, France, and the young United States—must not learn anything of these plans.

It was at this precise but awkward moment that John Evans of Waunfawr arrived in St. Louis, on his lone way

west—and with some wild, laughable story of wanting to
search for fair-skinned Indians who spoke Welsh. It was
evident at once to Trudeau and his colleagues that Evans
was not just the harmless fool his stated objective made him
appear. No, this young man was obviously a clever British
spy! And before he could quite know how it all happened,
Evans found himself in jail. And in jail he languished for
nearly two years.

During this period—1794 and 1795—the Missouri Company sent out two exploring expeditions, but they accomplished little. The first, under the command of Jean Bap-
tiste Truteau, a St. Louis schoolmaster who knew nothing
about exploration, cost the Company over fifty thousand
dollars, but failed to accomplish any of its aims. A second
one, dispatched in April of 1794 to locate and aid the first,
met with even greater disaster.

A third such expedition was just in the formative stage
when Evans was finally released from prison, for two reasons: first, the Spanish administration had quietly made in-
quiries concerning the Mandan tribe and, from what they
learned, decided there might be something to Evans' remarks about Welsh Indians living up the Missouri River.
Trudeau knew that long before Spanish explorers entered
the New World, there had been tales of white Indians living
on the prairies of the west. Second, and more important,
the Lieutenant-Governor and his fellow workers had con-
cluded that the prisoner could be very useful to them. A
prime objective of the Spaniards in controlling the west was
to seek out and win over to their cause the Mandan Indians.
Certainly, the services of a man who *might* be kin to them
and speak their language would be invaluable. Yet he was

British. But the Spanish government had always carefully distinguished between the Celts and the English. They knew the Welsh, the Scots, and the Irish had little love for the English; moreover, John Evans was embittered against the Welshmen living in the United States because of their lack of support for his mission. His former jailors now openly courted his favor. In short, John Evans quickly became a Spanish agent.

To head the third expedition, designed—as were the two failures—to explore and chart the territory, a necessary step prior to fort-building, the Spaniards selected one James Mackay. In company with some fellow Scotsmen, Mackay had for several years trapped in Canada, gaining considerable experience in laying out routes and organizing expeditions. Now he had decided to seek his fortune farther south. Inviting him to St. Louis and finding him to be very interested in the project, Trudeau first granted Mackay Spanish nationality, and then the lengthy title of Principal Explorer and Director of Indian Territory in the Spanish Missouri Company. Mackay and his party were to follow the Missouri River to its headwaters—exactly what John Evans wanted to do—in the hope that there they would find the source of a stream flowing to the Pacific. Evans, despite his utter lack of experience, was appointed second-in-command to Mackay.

Well-armed and with ample supplies and money, Mackay, Evans, and thirty other men set out in August of 1795. Their four boats were loaded with over fifty thousand dollars' worth of wares to trade to the Indians. The goods in the first vessel were meant for the savage Sioux, through whose territory they would need to pass. Merchandise in the second craft was intended for the Arikaras, while that in the third was for the Mandans. The materials in the fourth boat were to be saved for the unknown Indians of the Rocky Mountains, beyond the Mandans.

It was hard, slow work, rowing against the swift Missouri in such hot, humid weather. There were frequent storms. Leaks developed in the boats, and repairs delayed the journey for over six weeks. The mouth of the Platte River was not reached until October 14. They camped there for eleven days; then, early in November, they came to a village of Omaha Indians.

In fact, a full day before Mackay, Evans, and their party sighted the encampment, Black Bird, the incredible, despotic Omaha chief, set out to meet them. Though an object of great fear to his own and neighboring tribes, Black Bird —named Washingguhsahba in his own language—favored traders and, having heard that a man who knew his job was on the river, honored Mackay by thus advancing to meet him. Mackay, for his part, remembered well the story a trader had told him earlier.

Leaving St. Louis with a fine assortment of goods, this merchant reached the Omahas and asked Black Bird's permission to trade. The great chief was agreeable, but ordered the trader to carry all the goods into his lodge first. Puzzled, the trader complied. Next, Black Bird demanded that every package be opened for his personal inspection. That done, the chief slowly and carefully selected nearly a quarter of the choicest merchandise and moved it to another part of his lodge. He then turned to the bewildered trader and said, "Now, my son, the goods I have chosen are mine; the rest is yours. Don't worry—my people shall trade with you for your goods *at your own price.*" And Washing-guhsahba made good his word: he later called his herald, who climbed to the top of Black Bird's lodge and commanded the Indians, in the name of their fearsome chief, to bring their furs—beaver, otter, bear, muskrat, all—and not dispute the white man's exchanges. It turned out, the trader had said, concluding his tale, to be the most profitable voyage he had ever made.

Mackay also knew—he must have heard it many times back in St. Louis from the retired Indian agent, Tellier—the source of Black Bird's absolute power. The chief's prowess in war was clear to all; but the thing that made every Indian believe him possessed of supernatural powers was—arsenic! Some time ago, a white trader had sold him a quantity of this element and told him how to use it. If, afterwards, anyone dared oppose his will, Black Bird simply *prophesied* that brave's death within a certain brief time and then quietly brought it about. Once, he served poisoned food to sixty of his warriors at a great feast, assuring them beforehand that the Great Spirit had revealed to him that they would all die before morning. By the time Mackay and his men arrived, Black Bird's authority over his entire tribe—as well as other nearby ones—was unquestioned.

What Mackay and Evans couldn't know, of course, was that within five years the dread chief would be dead; a victim, along with many of his nation, of smallpox. Following his last request to the smallest detail—they would be afraid not to—Washingguhsahba's people buried him sitting astride his favorite horse. The horse—some say it was a mule—was led into the mouth of a cave atop a hill, high

above the Missouri River, about eighteen miles below the
Omaha village. There the animal was turned so that the
chief—who had seen so clearly the wave of the future—
faced east, toward the country of the white men. He
wanted, he had said, in death as in life to be able to greet
the white traders as they approached his land. The cave
was sealed with rocks, the customary burial mound erected
over it, and Black Bird's tyrannical reign was over.

What Mackay did see, and plainly, was that he and his
explorers would have to spend the winter among the
Omahas. Because of the unexpected delays, the expedition
was less than halfway to the Mandan country but already
there were raw, biting winds and heavy snow. At his
command, the men unloaded the four pirogues, their long
flat-bottomed boats, and—purchasing Black Bird's friendship with bolts of cloth, tobacco, kettles, blankets, medals,
and guns—set about building a fort. This, named Fort
Charles—Charles IV was King of Spain—was just a hut,
really, but the first in the proposed chain that would reach
to the Pacific, protecting the Spanish frontier against foreign encroachment.

When, before long, food became scarce, Mackay ordered
Evans and a few of the men to accompany some of the
Indians on a buffalo hunt. For twenty-five days on the
wide, flat prairie in bitter winter weather, Don Juan Evans,
as he was now called, hunted big game with red-skinned
savages. The rugged hills of his native Caernarvonshire and
the gentle, cozy Methodist parsonage must have seemed
even more than their half a world away.

When he returned to camp, Evans found Principal Explorer Mackay very excited. Word had just reached the

Scotsman that, sixteen months earlier, the North West Fur Company, the French operation now in British hands, had established a fort in the Mandan territory! This was bad news indeed, for if the British could maintain such a post they would block, right there, the hoped-for Spanish route from the Mississippi valley to the Pacific Ocean.

Cursing his luck, Mackay at once sent Evans and several of the men out on a scouting trip. Mackay's written instructions to the inexperienced Evans were explicit: his first duty was, of course, to drive the British out, but he was to mark the route carefully, recording the latitude and longitude daily as well as the wind direction, and make a detailed map as he proceeded. He was to take careful notes on the geographical and biological phenomena encountered: the mountains, streams, vegetation, and animals, as well as the varieties of Indians seen—being careful to avoid any on the warpath. He was to observe their religious rites and mode of life. Yet the Indians must never suspect he was spying on them; thus he was not to fire a gun, cut wood with a knife, or build a fire whose smoke would betray his presence. He should not camp too early in the evening, but must break before dawn. And when he happened upon an Indian village, he was to ground arms some distance away. He must never appear timid or fearful. Always he was to distribute his gifts sparingly, as the time of his return to Fort Charles could not be known. He was on no account to neglect his journal: "in case you will be short of ink use the powder, and for want of powder in the summer you will surely find some fruit whose juice can replace both."

When he reached the source of the Missouri, Evans was to inquire of the Indians there about westward-flowing

Buffalo chase, single death. Painting by George Catlin

rivers. And everywhere he went, he was to claim the land in the name of King Charles. Finally, his mission completed, Evans was to return down the Missouri to meet Mackay, who should—by that time—have reached the Mandans. If, by any chance, Evans found Mackay dead, or was unable to locate him, he was to continue on to St. Louis and turn in all his information—his map and his journals—to the Spanish government seated there.

In February then, of 1796, Evans and his party started; but they had gone less than three hundred miles—overland, since the river was frozen—when they were forced to turn back, all the way to Fort Charles, by a band of Sioux on the warpath. Evans bided his time until June 8. Setting out again, he began his journal afresh, and each day added a

Buffalo chase, with bows and arrows. Painting by George Catlin

bit to the map that was to guide Lewis and Clark many years later. The explorers proceeded up the Missouri through the Badlands of Dakota. After nine long weeks of fighting the river, greatly swollen by melting snow from the Rockies, they reached the Arikara Indians. Now Don Juan Evans, though but seven hundred miles from Fort Charles, was farther west than any Spaniard had pushed from an eastern base. The Arikaras demanded his supplies, but somehow Evans persuaded them to allow him and his men—and most of the goods—to continue on their way. It took him six precious weeks to do this; but that he did it at all, shows his merit.

On September 23 Evans reached a Mandan village, and was—possibly—the first white man to have broken the Sioux

and Arikara blockade. As instructed, he handed out his
medals, flags, and other gifts on behalf of the King of Spain.
The Mandans, in turn, ceremoniously welcomed him to their
homeland. Formalities ended, Evans moved quickly against
the British fur traders, and ousted them within five days.
He took possession of their fort, renaming it Fort Mackay,
then pulled down the Union Jack and raised the flag of
Spain in its stead. Again, Evans acted at an inopportune
time, for within two weeks Spain had declared war against
Great Britain. Having joined the Spaniards, Evans was now
guilty of treason and could never go home to Wales.

He spent the next six months with the Mandans—winter
months, with blizzards, cold snaps, and Arctic gales that
must have taken heavy toll on a body predisposed to tuber-
culosis. (John Evans' father had died its victim at the age
of forty-eight, just four years before young Evans left
home. And at this moment, unknown to him as he shivered
in the earth-covered lodge of Black Cat and Big White
Man, the two Mandan chiefs, his beloved brother Evan
lay dying in Waunfawr of the same disease.) Yet, whatever
the weather, Evans had ample time to observe the Indians
closely, to ask questions, to entertain them with his flute,
to learn—finally—whether or not they were the long-sought
tribe.

Were the Mandans the Welsh Indians? If not, it becomes
a bit difficult to understand how Evans so easily and so
quickly won them over to the Spanish side. True, he gave
them presents; but so had the British, and the Mandans—
as we shall see later—were a rich tribe; also, there is evidence they much preferred dealing with the British to the
Spanish. Yet Evans, seemingly, had but to ask them for

anything, and if they could provide it, it was his. Moreover, midway in his sojourn among them, they appear to have saved his life at the expense of profit to themselves. There are, however, two differing reports of this incident, and we should look at both.

In the depths of winter, when Evans was virtually alone with the Mandans and had almost nothing left to trade, the men of the North West Fur Company, whom he had driven out, suddenly returned—loaded with handsome goods. They were led by Réné Jessaume (his name is spelled a dozen different ways) an illiterate French-Canadian, now employed by the British, who had spent a lifetime on the upper Missouri as a guide and interpreter—and was so to serve Lewis and Clark, later. The raw, unskilled Evans can hardly have been a match for him, but exactly what ensued is not clear. In the archives of the Hudson's Bay Company—it soon absorbed the North West Company—we read: "Mr. Evans and the Canadians was almost at fisticuffs in attempting to prevent them from Trading with the natives, and not having goods himself [Evans] set all the Indians out against him [that is, Jessaume]."

Evans' own account, however, is that Jessaume and his party sought to wean the Indians from him and his few men with presents, then tried to persuade the Mandans to kill him. When the Indians refused, and warned Evans of his danger, Jessaume himself sneaked into Evans' dwelling. But before he could fire, the Mandans caught him, forcing him—with his men and all their beautiful merchandise—to flee. The Indians dragged Jessaume out by his heels and would, according to Evans, have executed him on the spot had not he—Evans—intervened. Why, unless the Mandans felt a deep kinship with the Welshman, should they have done this?

Before spring, the two Mandan chieftains, Big White Man and Black Cat, gave Evans detailed information concerning the Missouri River beyond their village. But with his supplies gone, he had no choice but to return to James Mackay and restock. Thus, in May of 1797, Evans left the Mandans, promising to come back with guns and ammunition, and headed down the Missouri. When he reached Fort Charles he learned that Mackay, just now absent on a trip into the Nebraska territory, had also been forced to turn back when his goods ran out, and—worse yet—the Spanish Missouri Company had gone bankrupt. The Mackay-Evans expedition ended because of lack of money.

Descending eighteen hundred miles on the swift-flowing river in only sixty-eight days, evading sand bars and countless small islands, Evans arrived back in St. Louis on July 15, 1797, nearly two years after leaving it. Following Mackay's final direction, he delivered his journal and the map he had drawn to the Spanish authorities. Thus ended John Evans' professional mission; his personal one was also complete—except for one detail.

To bring his long, self-imposed task to a finish, he wrote a note to Dr. Samuel Jones, the Welsh-American leader in Philadelphia. One sentence in that brief letter would seem to close forever the matter of the Welsh Indians: "In respect of the Welsh Indians, I have only to inform you that I could not meet with such a people; and from intercourse I have had with Indians from latitude 35 to 49 I think you may with safety inform our friends that they have no existence."

A portion of John Evans' map, showing the Mandan villages

Evans' terse language is plain enough: he found no trace
of the Welsh Indians anywhere along the Missouri. Or did
he, and did he now lie about it? Remember that Evans
could not go back to Wales, and seemingly had no desire
to return to Philadelphia or Baltimore. Disgusted with the
Welsh-Americans' lack of financial support of his quest,
he had thrown in his lot with the Spanish, and an examination of the facts shows he was well paid. By now Evans,
weakened by his long venture, was also an alcoholic, inef-
ficient and unreliable in his employment; yet the Spanish
government in St. Louis immediately offered him a position
as a land surveyor, an assurance of security for life—with a
down payment, equal to two thousand dollars, in cash. This
was a very large sum of money in 1797.

It seems likely that Evans wrote his short letter, denying
the existence of the Welsh Indians, at the behest of the
Spaniards; and that it was for this—rather than his journal
and map, or surveying services—that he was so generously
rewarded. What better evidence could the Spanish have,
to refute any British claim to Mandan territory, than the
written signed statement of a native Welshman who had
come to America for no other purpose than to determine
whether or not the Welsh Indians existed?

Weight is lent to this theory—and it must remain just a
theory—by the written memorandum of an acquaintance:
" . . . when heavily in strong liquor [Evans] bragged to his
friends in St. Louis that the Welsh Indians would keep
their secret to their graves because he had been hand-
somely paid to keep quiet on the subject. He added that
in a few more years there would be no more trace of any
Welsh ancestry or language as time and disease would

eventually remove all traces." The great smallpox epidemic of 1837, exactly forty years later, did indeed practically wipe out the Mandans. And, though it was to be expected that with increased contact between Indians and white men the natives would succumb to the traders' and explorers' illnesses—they could build no immunity to them—taken in context, Evans' statement—if he made it—seems more prophetic than drunken raving.

Evans' health continued to decline. He went to Louisiana, where he became a member of the household of Don Manuel Gayoso de Lemos, the new Governor of New Orleans. Why was this? Did Don Manuel have orders to see that Evans was cared for? And did not talk too freely? At least, we know that the Governor authored a document stating: "It is in the interests of His Catholic Majesty that the reports of British Indians in Mandan country be denied once and for all. If, however, as seems possible, the subject of association with the Mandans is not mentioned by the British, it might be more expedient to refrain from referring to this tribe, but to relate the denial only to the Padoucas who have already been said by the British to have an association with the Welsh."

Is more proof of Evans' perfidy needed? Or was he instead a disappointed, broken, truth-telling man? We will never know; for in either case he took everything he learned—or did not learn—about the Welsh-speaking Indians to his own early grave. In May of 1799, ravaged with disease and with his mind blurred, John Thomas Evans of Waunfawr, adventurer, opportunist, traitor—but mapmaker extraordinary and, it may be, finder of the Welsh Indians—was dead at the age of twenty-nine.

CHAPTER 6

The Search Continues

BELIEF IN THE EX-
istence of Welsh Indians somewhere west of the Mississippi
River continued, despite John Evans' flat statement to the
contrary. And if the Welsh in Pennsylvania, led by Pritchard and Jones, had felt personal investigation foolhardy, a
flourishing Welsh colony in Oneida County, New York, did
not. The years 1795 to 1800, the period of Evans' sojourn
and death, had seen many, many immigrants from Wales
moving into this area, by way of Philadelphia, and settling
chiefly in Utica and Steuben. (Even today, Utica is the
acknowledged "Welsh capital" of the United States.)

These Oneida County Welshmen were determined to
seek out the American descendants of Madog; and early in
the spring of 1819, James Owen of Trenton wrote to a
friend back in Wales: "I think, if we live a little longer, the
door will be opened for us to find out about the old Kymry
[Welsh people]. We here are determined to make every
effort to find them out. We are almost sure that they may
be found on the Mud river, twelve miles from the Missouri.
Next week we are to collect money to send a man to them.

We have many ready to go, but we have decided to send John T. Roberts, who was born near Denbigh [in Wales]. . ."

The John Roberts referred to was, at that time, a contractor on the Erie Canal—well qualified for the search and eager to get on with it. As his companion, he chose a young man—Welsh, of course—named William Parry.

The two men left Utica on April 14, 1819, and proceeded west, reaching Pittsburgh, Pennsylvania, early in May. There they met Major Stephen H. Long, the noted explorer, who had just been commissioned by the United States government to investigate the vast region south of the Missouri River. Long was interested in Roberts' and Parry's quest, and told them that it was the opinion of William Clark—of the Lewis and Clark expedition, and now governor of the Missouri Territory—that the Welsh Indians lived near the Rocky Mountains. Greatly encouraged, the two Welshmen, traveling part of the time with Major Long and his party, reached St. Louis on the twenty-eighth of May, and began an intensive inquiry among the Indian traders there. They wanted to determine the exact location of the Welsh Indians before going any farther.

Roberts and Parry discussed their subject endlessly with countless men familiar with the languages of the western Indians. All denied ever having met with "white" or Welsh-speaking Indians, though almost all had heard of them and had expected to see them.

In addition to the professional interpreters whom they interviewed, the Oneida County men saw, in St. Louis, upon different occasions, a number of Indians from various tribes; and each time, the Welshmen spoke carefully to them in Welsh. But invariably—one report states—the Indians "put their fingers in their ears."

Realizing they were getting nowhere, Parry went seven hundred miles up the Missouri—the same distance covered by John Evans—while Roberts stayed on in St. Louis and advertised. He went to a newspaper office, and persuaded the editor to run some articles about Prince Madog's discovery of America, together with a few of the more colorful accounts of the Welsh Indians. Then, interest aroused, the newspaper announced that two Welshmen had come all the way to St. Louis in search of such Indians, and requested anyone with information about them to produce it.

Roberts later reported his and Parry's experience—in the Welsh-American journal, *Seren Gomer*—and stated that this advertisement appeared in a newspaper covering hundreds of miles, "even to New Orleans, near the Gulf of Mexico," but that there had been no response.

In the meantime, Parry returned. He, too, had found nothing.

This was all very disappointing, but more discouragement was to follow. Soon Roberts came upon Major Amos Stoddard's *History of the Western Parts of America*, wherein it said that Indians speaking the Welsh language lived on the Arkansas and Red Rivers, and were known as Ietans or Alitans. Ever diligent, and filled with fresh enthusiasm, Roberts sought out men who claimed they understood the speech of this tribe; but not one word of Welsh did they comprehend.

In all, Roberts remained in St. Louis two years. At last, convinced that the Welsh Indians were not to be found on the Missouri River, yet maintaining his belief in their existence, he drifted west to Sacramento, California, where he lived past the age of ninety.

Parry's fate is not known, but thirty-five years later we hear again from John Roberts. It came about this way:

In March of 1856 a letter appeared in *Y Cenhadwr*, a Welsh monthly magazine published at Steuben, back in Oneida County, New York, asking that another expedition to search for the Welsh Indians be financed and sent out from the county. The "white" Indians were even now, the correspondent felt sure, "talking in the dear old language and holding Eisteddfods [harping, singing, and verse-making contests] somewhere in the northwest."

Evidently a subscriber to the magazine, John Roberts— in faraway Sacramento—immediately replied to the letter. Under date of July 16, Roberts wrote that a Richard P. Pierce, originally from Anglesey in North Wales, had crossed America overland, with a small party, from Wisconsin to California. After passing the Great Salt Lake, Roberts continues, Pierce and his group met another Welshman in the company of some Indians. This man had left Wales when young, arrived in New Orleans, joined forces with some fur traders, and married an Indian squaw. Pierce reported the man as saying there was a tribe of "white" Indians about two days' journey to the south who spoke Welsh. This other Welshman, Roberts says, told Pierce "great tales" of these people, and offered to lead him and his party to them. Unfortunately, here Roberts' letter ends, without even divulging his source of information except for stating that it was not Pierce himself; that he, Roberts, had been unsuccessful in getting in direct touch with Pierce.

A bit more than a year later, on November 17, 1857, John Roberts again wrote a letter to *Y Cenhadwr*. This time he reported that a Mr. Gilman had been visiting him. Gil-

man, it seems, had spent the winter of 1852-53 in Salt Lake
City. During this period, he had occasion to call upon an old
lady and her daughter, some forty miles away. While he
was there, three very light-complexioned Indians stopped by
—a woman and two young lads. To Gilman's surprise, they
and the old woman conversed merrily, in a language unknown to him, for a time. When the Indians left, the aged
one told Gilman the language was Welsh!

Roberts concludes his sketchy letter by saying, "Mr.
Gilman had never heard of Madog ab Owain Gwynedd.
In my opinion this is stronger proof of the existence of the
Welsh Indians than anything I have seen before; and I
think there is little doubt but they could be found. If I had
had such information as this when I was in St. Louis looking for them in 1819, I would have been able to find them.
There were but few Welsh people in America then compared to what there are now; and the collection made was
not more than enough to pay two men's expenses to St.
Louis and back. We could get no information of them then,
and went no further. I think they could be found now without much difficulty."

Despite John Roberts' reluctance to surrender his conviction in the face of repeated disappointment, we have
to classify his and Parry's search as a complete failure. And
it was, so far as is known, the last organized effort made
to locate the elusive tribe.

But let us turn now to the dream-ridden genius who—
though not specifically searching for them—said, loudly and
in print, that he did, indeed, find the Welsh Indians.

 CHAPTER 7

George Catlin and
the Mandans

GEORGE CATLIN WAS
the man who said he found the Welsh Indians, and the
tribe was the Mandans. How these two came together—
the cultured, sensitive young lawyer-artist from Pennsylvania and the tribe of about sixteen hundred savages living along the Heart River, a tributary of the great Missouri
—forms one of the more romantic, but true, tales of the early
nineteenth century.

As the third son and fifth child of fourteen born to Putnam Catlin, successful lawyer and comfortable country
squire, George Catlin began life on July 26, 1796, in the
riverfront town of Wilkes-Barre, Pennsylvania. From baby-
hood, he heard tales of Indian life, though the Indians
themselves had left the area some time ago. When she was
but seven years old, his mother, Polly Sutton Catlin, had
been captured at the surrender of Forty Fort during the
terrible Wyoming Valley massacre. Later, she was released

unharmed. Her father, George's grandfather, had barely escaped death by swimming the Susquehanna beneath a shower of Indian arrows. Frontiersmen, explorers, fur trappers, and Indian fighters—all were frequent callers at Putnam Catlin's Broome County, New York, plantation. (The family had moved across the Pennsylvania border soon after George's birth.) Far into the night the visitors would talk, while young George listened eagerly. Once, a stray Oneida whom his father befriended gave the lad an iron tomahawk, ground to gleaming brightness. George quickly mastered the art of throwing it, but one of his playmates was not so dexterous, and Catlin carried the resulting scar all his life. A poor throw caused the weapon to glance off a tree; the sharp blade sliced deep into George's left cheek.

But Indian affairs were almost forgotten when, in 1817, young Catlin entered America's first law school, kept by Judge Tapping Reeve in Litchfield, Connecticut. Litchfield was a rich cultural center of the period: Lyman Beecher was preaching his eloquent sermons while his young daughter, to become known to all the world as Harriet Beecher Stowe, the author of *Uncle Tom's Cabin,* watched and listened admiringly. Anson Dickinson was painting his fine miniatures and Ralph Earle his portraits. There was good music, too, and stimulating conversation. George Catlin absorbed it all; he passed his bar examinations and moved— in 1820—to Philadelphia, possessed of some knowledge of the law, but with greater interest in painting, together with the polished manners he was to display equally in the bare, earthy lodges of Indian chiefs and the luxurious drawing rooms of Europe's kings.

In Philadelphia, Catlin practiced no law but devoted himself to painting, dividing his leisure hours between the exhibition rooms of the Pennsylvania Academy of Art and Charles Willson Peale's amazing Philadelphia Museum. In the latter, Catlin would hurry past the hundreds of mounted specimens of every obtainable animal, bird, fish, insect, ore, and mineral, as well as a choice mastodon skeleton, to linger over the examples of Indian handicraft and, especially, a few portraits of Indians. These he studied, comparing them to his vivid childhood recollection of the warrior who had given him the tomahawk.

Then one day, in the Museum's great hall, he stared in wonder as a richly clad, painted, and feathered delegation of western tribal chiefs, on their way home from making an appeal to the government in Washington, D.C., were being shown, by Peale himself, the Museum's treasures. From that moment on, George Catlin had a mission and a destiny. He would, he told himself, record on canvas, for future generations to see, the vanishing American Indian. He would go west; not only to paint, but to write the Indians' history—while there was yet time. And he would have his own museum: a traveling collection of everything Indian; everything he could gather together—animal, mineral, or vegetable—that had affected Indian life and culture. Then, with his paintings and his curios he would tour the world, so that all men might see and know America's heritage. Catlin became a man with a cause, a man obsessed.

But he had no money to finance his dream. Also, he would have to develop an entirely different style of painting, and this would take time. He had, in the three years since leaving Litchfield, made a name for himself painting miniatures in water color on ivory. It was slow, meticulous work. Now he began to practice painting rapidly, in oils on canvas, life-sized portraits, though continuing to earn his living by the miniatures. Through a mutual friend, Catlin was introduced to DeWitt Clinton, the Governor of New York and sponsor of the Erie Canal. Clinton took to the young man at once; Catlin did a series of official portraits of the Governor, at good fees, and—through him— was able to paint some eastern Indians employed in constructing the Canal.

It was during this period of association with DeWitt Clinton that Catlin met and married Clara Bartlett Gregory, daughter of a wealthy Albany landowner.

Meanwhile, time was wasting. Already legislation was before Congress that would move the eastern Indians across the Mississippi. Their nearness would, inevitably, alter the life of the western tribes. The newly developed steamboat and the coming of the railroad would take hordes of white emigrants into the Indians' midst, destroying their way of life. He must leave his wife, his family, his promising career and head west—*now*.

And he did just that. Settling his wife—slowly recovering from a serious illness—in her father's house, George Catlin reached St. Louis in the spring of 1830. He proceeded at once to the Indian Office. Here it was that General William Clark administered Indian affairs in the vast western territory—from Canada to Mexico, from the Mississippi River to the Pacific coast—and without his permission no white man could legally explore, trap fur, or trade anywhere in the entire region.

The crusty old explorer, in his soiled buckskins and be-

William Clark, painted by Charles W. Peale

draggled coonskin cap, was not overly impressed with the
letters of introduction Catlin presented; but he was won
over as soon as Catlin unrolled a few of his portraits of the
eastern Indians. Clark—who did admirable pen drawings
himself—responded at once to the younger man's respect
and concern for, as well as fascination with, the western Indians; and he readily agreed that time was running out for
their civilization. Soon Catlin's easel stood in a corner of
the General's conference room; and while Clark and the
Indians parleyed, Catlin's brush flew.

So the weeks and months passed. By day he sketched
or painted, either in the Office or down at the water-
front warehouse where the visiting Indian delegations were

housed. At night he bombarded Clark, who knew as much
or more about Indian life and customs than any other white
man alive, with questions.

From time to time, Clark would take the eager artist
along on expeditions into the surrounding Indian country,
and thus Catlin painted the Iowas, Missouris, Sioux, Omahas, Sacs, Foxes, Delawares, Kickapoos, Potawatomies,
Weas, Peorias, Shawanoes, and Kaskaskias. Once, he and
the General went upriver as far as the Kansa encampment,
and Catlin was speechless with delight. Uncorrupted as yet
by contact with white men, this colorful tribe was more
what he was seeking. The braves had scalps and bearclaws
dangling from their waists; their heads were crested with
tufts of dyed deer's hair and bright feathers. Not for them
the brass-buttoned frock coats, nor the government-issued
derby hats still wrapped in brown paper and tied with
green string that the Indians around St. Louis considered
so elegant. Proud and independent, the Kansas had not
learned to ape the white man nor to beg from him. Catlin
yearned to go on, to more distant tribes.

And so, on March 26 of 1832, he boarded the steamboat
Yellowstone, owned by the American Fur Company, making her first trip up the Missouri. At Fort Union, terminus
of the voyage at the mouth of the Yellowstone River, Catlin
disembarked. Kenneth McKenzie, captain of the fort, also
owned by the American Fur Company and the largest and
best-equipped trading post in the West, provided him
with generous quarters in a blockhouse; and he happily
painted the few sturdy Blackfeet, so named because they
wore black moccasins, and the tall—some were six foot six
—Crows he could induce to sit for him.

George Catlin in 1849. Portrait by William Fisk

Then, with two companions, Catlin began the nearly two thousand-mile descent, in a canoe, back to St. Louis—stopping for lengthy periods to visit and paint ten more tribes. Of these, the most important were the Mandans; and to them Catlin devoted most of his time. He became convinced, by the many ways in which they differed from any other tribe, that the Mandans were the long-sought Welsh Indians.

But if Catlin was the last white man to have close contact with the Mandans, he was far from the first to discover the things that set them apart.

The first to visit what is now North Dakota and leave a journal of his travels was the French explorer and agent of a Canadian fur company, Pierre Gaultier de Varennes, Sieur de la Vérendrye, who began the lengthy trip across country from Portage la Prairie in the fall of 1738. On the way, he was told by the Assiniboine Indians that when— and if—he reached the Mandans, a tribe almost unknown at that time, he would see a people white like himself!

Fortunately, La Vérendrye was a careful observer and copious note-taker; and in addition to their appearance, which we shall examine later, he found the Mandans' customs and mode of living different from those of any other tribe he met.

First of all, they were not nomadic hunters. A sedentary tribe, the Mandans lived in fixed villages for long periods of time, and farmed. There is archaeological evidence that, at the time of La Vérendrye's visit, they had lived on the Missouri River for many years; and while it is not entirely clear how they got there, there is good reason for believing they had earlier occupied a portion of the Ohio Valley. In support of this, La Vérendrye—in his fifteen-page report— says that a Mandan chief told him that the ancestors of his tribe were the first human inhabitants in that area; that they had formerly lived much farther south, but had been driven north and west by their enemies.

Be that as it may, by 1738 the Mandan nation—numbering about fifteen thousand—was established in several permanent villages, well laid out in clean, neat streets and squares! And their houses—130 in the smaller villages, up to a thousand in all—were not simple wigwams, but lasting, beehive-shaped, earth-covered lodges, built to a regular plan.

For protection against floodwaters the villages were situated on headlands, overlooking the river; for defense against human enemies—the Arikaras and Cheyennes—they were surrounded by pickets. La Vérendrye also mentions seeing trenches, and a later French explorer, Bougainville, states that the villages were always surrounded by moats.

For their food, the Mandans—unlike other tribes—depended upon raising crops, fishing, and hunting small game. (Buffalo were, of course, taken any time of the year they were sighted in the neighborhood; but this tribe did not go off on long hunting trips, as other Indians did.) The land around the Mandan villages—smooth river bottom— was very productive, making fertilization unnecessary, and extremely easy to work, requiring only the crudest implements to cultivate it. Generally just a hoe, fashioned from the shoulder blade of a buffalo or elk, trimmed, and then fastened with thongs to a crooked stick, was used. Mainly the tribe raised corn, beans, squash, melons, sunflowers (the seeds are edible), and a little tobacco; crops well suited to the cold, dry climate of the region. Their success in farming is demonstrated by the fact that they frequently traded their corn and tobacco to northern, unagricultural tribes for guns, kettles, tools, and cloth. (The northern Indians had gotten these items from white traders, of course.) In all things, the Mandans were a prosperous and powerful tribe until 1772, or a bit later, when their long troubles began.

Concerning the "whiteness" of the tribe, La Vérendrye was not as impressed as later visitors, saying only that "the men are stout and tall—with a good physiognomy. The women have not the Indian physiognomy." He was the first of many, however, to note the astounding fact that the Mandan men grew beards and the older people had "grey hair." Indians—other Indians—were beardless and did not turn gray.

The next known caller was John Evans, who denied— for his own reasons—that the Mandans were the Welsh Indians, though by the time he reached them the centuries would have diminished evidence of such origin. Only a keen observer of *many* Indian tribes, such as Catlin, would have detected the Mandans' significant differences, which were to convince him of their Welsh blood.

Hard upon Evans' heels came another Welshman, David Thompson, who left a vivid description of his adventure. Acting as Thompson's guide on the journey was Jessaume —he who had, just a few months earlier, tried to kill John Evans and had been set upon by the Mandans.

At first it seems remarkable that, in his journal, Thompson does not mention Evans' earlier visit. Surely, the Man-

Mink, a beautiful Mandan girl. Painting by George Catlin

dans would have told him about it, Thompson being a
Welshman and Evans' countryman? But maybe it isn't so
strange after all. The Indians, even though of Welsh ancestry, might well not recognize Thompson as a corrupted
Welsh surname. Then too, Thompson seemingly knew little
about Wales, and may never even have heard of Prince
Madog or the Welsh Indians. True, his grandfather had
been David ap Thomas; but when the grandfather's son—
David Thompson's father—moved to London, he anglicized
the name to Thompson. David, the explorer, was thus born
in London. His father died when he was a small child; and
he very probably never saw Wales or heard Welsh spoken,
for at the age of fourteen he was apprenticed to the Hudson's Bay Company and shipped to Canada.

But if David Thompson had no cause to suspect he was
among the Welsh Indians, he does tell us that at the time
of his visit—1798—the Mandans lived in but five villages.
The smallpox, their greatest enemy and the one which was
soon to annihilate them, plus wars with neighboring tribes
had greatly reduced their numbers since the days of La
Vérendrye.

The next to call upon this unique nation, in point of time,
were Meriwether Lewis and William Clark, who spent the
fall and winter of 1804 at Fort Mandan. Their account of
this is very full, but the details are scattered among a mass
of other material. Of particular interest here is the fact that
a later historian, Frederick Steines, tells us that "when the
seventy-year-old General Clark spoke of the daughters of
the Mandan his eyes beamed with youthful fire and he answered me that they were the handsomest women in the
world." Clark's enthusiastic opinion was shared by other

Mah-to-toh-pa (Four Bears), a Mandan second chief. Painting by George Catlin

Another Catlin portrait of Mah-to-toh-pa. At this time he was in mourning; thus, he is undressed, has cut a few locks of his hair, and formed the rest into plaits with glue and red paint.

white explorers, each of whom cited the women's blue eyes, fair complexions, and blonde or reddish hair.

Following Lewis and Clark came—in 1806—Alexander Henry, a trader for the North West Fur Company. He, too, kept a fairly full journal, but gave no really new information. In 1811, Henry M. Brackenridge and John Bradbury visited the tribe. Each later published a report of his journey; but again, there was little in them that added to La Vérendrye's notes, though Brackenridge, speaking of the Mandan chief, Big White Man, who was six feet, ten inches tall, describes him as "a fine looking Indian, and very intelligent—his complexion fair, very little different from that of a white man much exposed to the sun . . ."

The seventh and eighth—and last—white men to dwell for any length of time among the Mandan nation were the lawyer-artist George Catlin, and then a German nobleman, Maximilian, Prince of Wied-Neuwied, who was to spend part of the winter of 1833-34 with them.

Catlin, too, had been told before he ever left St. Louis that the Mandans were a very strange people, half white. His informant was, of course, his mentor, the superintendent of the Indian agency, William Clark. Arriving at the Mandan villages in the spring of 1833, Catlin saw no reason to disagree with the great explorer's statement.

In his book on the North American Indians, published much later, Catlin stresses—naturally enough, for these are the things he could paint—their physical differences. The Mandans were, he said, completely distinct from any other tribe. Alexander Henry, some years earlier, had written that in general this tribe did not have the coarse hair of Indians; that it was finer, more dark brown than black, and that a few had fair hair. Their eyes, he continued, were

*Ha-na-ta-nu-nauk (Wolf Chief), head chief of the Mandans.
Painting by George Catlin*

not black as usual, but brown or sometimes even gray. Catlin, with his artist's eye, speaks instead of their "many"
shades of complexion and hair; saying further that the
women frequently had white skin with hazel, blue, or gray
eyes. Indeed, his portraits of Mandan women show beauti-
fully chiseled faces; large, bright blue eyes; well-shaped,
somewhat long noses; and thin, cupid's-bow lips.

Maximilian, coming right after Catlin, took particular
pains to ridicule the theory of the tribe's white origin and
especially its Welsh ancestry. But even he admits their
peculiarity among Indians. Although usually brown or cop-
per-colored, some Mandans were yellow or white-ish, he
grants. Further, he says that when clean a number were
nearly white, with rosy cheeks. He describes long coarse
hair, usually black; but does add that many children had
brown hair, and there were families with gray hair.

Summing up the constantly cited physical characteristics,
there can be no doubt that a tendency to light complexion
existed among the Mandans, and all of the authorities—
even Maximilian—express the opinion that this was not from
contact with the white explorers and traders. Hjalmar Rued
Holand, noted historian, says "all archaeologists are agreed
that the Mandan Indians have been in prehistoric contact
with Europeans. Their frequently recurring blue eyes and
their blonde complexion and their superior culture prove
this." In connection with the emphasis on blondeness, it
should be pointed out that most Welsh are dark eyed and
dark haired. This fact, however, need not negate the Mandans being the Welsh Indians. Far from it; we now have
reason to believe, largely through the discovery in Minne-

sota of the Kensington Stone with its runic inscriptions, that
Norsemen crossed our continent in the fourteenth century.
May they not have mingled with the Mandans, of Welsh
origin, bequeathing to some their Nordic blue eyes and
blonde locks? Certainly this is in accordance with Men-
delian laws and is a possibility, if not a probability.

One of the differences which intrigued Catlin and the
other visitors was the Mandan fishing craft. "They fished,"
Catlin writes, "in a boat which was unlike any used by other
Indian tribes in America. It was made of willow or other
flexible boughs which formed a frame shaped like a round
tub. Buffalo skins were stretched underneath the frame. It
was exactly like the coracle used in Wales and was operated
in the same manner. The woman carried the tub on her
shoulders to the river. Stepping into it, she propelled it by
inserting a paddle into the water in front of her and drawing the paddle toward her, instead of using oars at the side
as was usual in the Indian canoes."

This technique is precisely that used by Wales' coracle-
men to this day. When not fishing, the man will paddle over
the fore end of the boat, either in a figure-eight motion, or
a scooping gesture. Catlin, keener-eyed than the rest, also
noted that the paddle bore a claw at the top of its loom;
this makes it identical to the paddle used—still—on the River
Teifi in Wales.

But if the similarity—identity, really—of the Welsh and
Mandan fishing boats and methods astonished Catlin, what
would have been his reaction had he known the Welsh language? Let us compare a few Welsh and Mandan fishing
terms:

Item	Mandan Word	Welsh Word	Welsh Pronunciation
coracle	koorig	corwg	kôr'ōog
paddle	ree	rhwyf	rhōo'ĭv
fishing area	burra	bwrw	bōo'rōo
fishing net	ruydrat	rhwyd rhwth	rōo'ĭd rōoth
fish (noun)	pisg	pysg	pŭsg

In any case, such a craft would have enabled the Mandans to fish more effectively than other tribes, though for
lengthy river trips the boat was slower than the usual Indian
canoe. We know that the Mandans also had large dugout
canoes—Catlin sketched them; but being easy to make and
carry, the ancient coracle was retained and used.

In the white explorers' journals there is frequent mention
of the gorgeous costumes the Mandans made and wore on
state occasions; and over and over again we hear of the
lovely blue beads they used. Says Catlin, "These people
have an extraordinary art of manufacturing a very beautiful
and lasting kind of blue glass bead, which they wear in
great quantities and value above all others that are brought
amongst them by fur-traders." The method of making these
beads was a closely guarded secret of the Mandan nation.
"This secret," continues Catlin, "is not only one that fur-
traders did not introduce amongst them, but one that I cannot learn from them."

There is but one reason for regarding the manufacture of
these beautiful blue beads as a clue to the Mandans' Welsh
ancestry. A study of the history of Lundy Isle reveals that
in ancient times a very similar blue glass bead was made
there and, seemingly, used as a form of currency. We remember that Meiron stated positively that the second, col-

onizing, expedition of Prince Madog departed from the Isle of Lundy. Did the colonists pick up some of the blue beads —and, more important, the secret of their manufacture— while awaiting a favorable wind?

A few other, much less striking, traits and customs of the Mandans that helped confirm Catlin's belief in their European—Welsh—origin could be listed:

Though as warlike as neighboring tribes, the Mandans seldom took male prisoners of war; and if they did, such prisoners were never tortured.

Surrounded by slave-holding tribes, the Mandans kept none. The Arikara, for instance, had a regular slavery system, and so did the Crows.

Every white visitor who left a journal comments at one time or another on the Mandans' hospitality and liberality.

Maximilian, as well as Catlin, was impressed by the Mandans' aesthetic sense. "Many of them take a real pleasure in music and painting and are very skillful in both . . . very fine orators . . . they like to talk."

To conclude the matter, it can be said that in general culture the Mandans were superior; they were far advanced in the arts of manufacture—their pottery was particularly outstanding—and they enjoyed more comforts, luxuries even, than other Indian nations.

For all these reasons, Catlin left the Mandans—in August of 1833—convinced, and he never wavered in this conviction, that he had found the descendants of Prince Madog and his colonists.

We have said that Catlin knew no Welsh, though he had doubtless heard it spoken by the Welsh miners in the coal country around Wilkes-Barre. We return now to this matter of language, as our last point of evidence, before describing the tragic end of both this extraordinary tribe and its best interpreter, Catlin.

Present-day linguistic scholars express opposing views concerning the similarity between Welsh and any Indian language. One group holds that the dialect of some Indian tribe, or tribes, was identical to Welsh. We have already heard testimony to this fact: Morgan Jones' narrative of how speaking Welsh to a brave saved his life; Stedman's adventure; Lieutenant Roberts' dining room encounter with the Indian chief; Abraham Chaplain's experience at Kaskaskia—all these people, and many more, agreed on this point. Surely they could not all have been mistaken? Or liars?

The other group holds that there is no similarity whatsoever between Welsh and any known Indian dialect, and there never was; that any *seeming* likeness is only coincidental. To those of this view, one must concede that no trace of Welsh exists in any Indian tongue *today*. But does that mean that there never was such a similarity?

We know that many years before either John Evans or George Catlin visited the Mandans, a trader named James Girty compiled a *Welsh-Indian Vocabulary* of over 350 words, phrases and brief sentences. Later, he linked these "Welsh Indians" with the Mandan tribe. Girty, seemingly an unsavory character, was born, along with his three brothers, Simon, George, and Thomas, near Harrisburg, Pennsylvania, in 1743. When his father—an intemperate Irish immigrant trader—was killed by Indians in 1756, James and his young brothers were taken captive.

Seehk-hee-de (White Eye-brows), a Mandan with yellow hair. Painting by George Catlin

Sha-ko-ka (The Mint), a Mandan girl with gray hair. Painting by George Catlin

Girty, adopted by and thoroughly identified throughout
his life with the Shawnees—he lived with them, fought with
them against the colonists, married one of them—became
an interpreter as well as a trader.

He was, of course, not Welsh; and where and how he
learned the language is unknown, as is how he knew any
Mandans. But when he met Francis Lewis, the New York
merchant and signer of the Declaration of Independence,
the two men conversed in Welsh. We don't have to take
Girty's word for this; Lewis himself recorded meeting the
renegade trader, and his great surprise that he, Girty, spoke
Welsh.

James Girty was not a linguist; he had no formal school-
ing, but—evidently—a flair for language. Thus he set down
only a word list, a vocabulary, making no attempt to compare grammatical constructions or sentence structures,
which would have helped later investigators so much. What
he did is of intense interest, nonetheless. A few of the words
and phrases he recorded follow, with an approximation of
the Welsh pronunciation.

English	"Welsh-Indian"	Welsh	Welsh Pronunciation
beautiful	prydfa	prydferth	prŭd′vĕrth
blue	glas	glas	glăss
bread	bara	bara	bä′rä
bridge	pont	pont	pônt
cow	buch	buwch	bĭ′ōōk
dance	dansio	dawnsio	dă′ōōn•sēo
estuary	aber	aber	ă′bĕr
father	taid	tad	tăd
foot	troed	troed	troid

English	"Welsh-Indian"	Welsh	Welsh Pronunciation
great	mawr	mawr	mä′ōor
harp	tefyn	telyn	těl′ĭn
he	efo	efo	ěv′ō
he is	ym-eff	y mae ef	ŭh mī′ěv
high	uchaf	uchel	ŭk′l
I	me	mi	mē
I am	yr-effi	yr wyfi	ŭr ōo′ĭv•ē
in the boat	in y kook	yn y cwch	ŭn ŭh kōok
milk	faeth	llaeth	tlä′ěth
night	nostogr	nos	nōss
old	hen	hen	hān
river	nant	nant	nănt
she	ea-ah	hi	hē
sing	canu	canu	kăn′ĭ
stone	kraig	carreg	kăr′rěg
thanks	dyawf	diolch	dē′ŏlk
to belong	pertin	perthyn	pěrth′ĭn
to cross	crocsi	croesi	krois′ĭ
valley	koom	cwm	kōom
water	duah	dŵr	dōor
we	noo	ni	nē
woodsmen	coedig	coedwig	koid•ōo′ĭg
you	nehi	chwi	kōo′ē
you are	yor-iddich-ni	yr ydych chwi	ŭr ŭdĭk kōo′ē

Girty's list, it should be emphasized, was compiled nearly sixty years prior to Catlin's visit. During these years the tribe itself had undergone revolutionary changes: their numbers had been decimated by deaths from diseases; surviving members had intermarried with other tribes; there were increased contacts with white traders. Naturally enough, these changes were reflected in the language—new elements being introduced, old terms becoming obsolete. For example, by Catlin's time "river" in the Mandan tongue had become *passah la*, not *nant*; "night" was *estogr* rather than *nostogr*; and the word for "foot" was *shee* instead of *troed*.

The language puzzle remains—and doubtless will remain —unsolved. That there is sufficient similarity to suggest a close link between the Welsh and Mandan tongues, in an earlier age, seems clear; but too much unlikeness exists for this to be proved.

In all, Catlin spent eight years among the western Indians, with only brief trips east to see his family or recover from bouts of illness. During this time, he painted over five hundred portraits of North American Indians from forty-eight tribes, made innumerable sketches, and collected thousands of artifacts. All these he then exhibited as "Catlin's Indian Gallery" in the larger American cities, beginning with Pittsburgh and Cincinnati, progressing to Buffalo and New York, then Philadelphia, Baltimore and Washington. His exhibition, a full train carload in bulk, was neither easy nor inexpensive to transport. And just the proper hanging of the paintings in each rented hall took days. The constant lecturing soon took its toll on Catlin's ever frail health; yet he persevered.

It was time now to go abroad, to fulfill his dream of showing *all* men what he could of this little-appreciated, vanishing civilization. So, in November of 1839, leaving his aged father, his wife Clara, and his little daughter, he sailed, with his nephew and eight tons of cargo—including two grizzly bears—for Liverpool, England. A rainy night's train ride brought them all to London and the leased Egyptian Hall in Piccadilly. The "show" ran for months, and was most enthusiastically received by Queen Victoria and the general public.

Nearly two years later, in October of 1841, still in London, Catlin published his monumental two-volume work, *Letters and Notes on the Manners, Customs and Condition of the North American Indians.* Sixteen of its fifty-eight chapters are devoted to the Mandans.

Yet long before Catlin's book came off the press, the Mandan Indians were all but extinct. In the summer of 1836, less than three years after Catlin's departure, more white traders had come up the Missouri River and its tributaries. Arriving at the Mandan settlement, they invited the village chiefs to come down to the boat and inspect the goods to be traded. Two members of the ship's crew were sick, but it is believed the captain did not know the nature of their illness. "Otherwise," wrote Catlin later, "he could not have been so cruel, so ill-advised as to [re]introduce smallpox among the Mandans."

Soon the disease spread to the villages on the east side of the river, and by 1837 it had engulfed the entire Mandan nation. Some victims threw themselves over the thirty-foot cliffs into the river. Only about 125 survived or, for some reason, did not get the disease; these were taken captive by the neighboring Ricarees, who then moved into the empty Mandan lodges. Many of the captive Mandans—made slaves —committed suicide. Thirteen years later, the census of 1850 recorded 385 Mandans living, but nearly all were of mixed blood; and well over a hundred years later, in 1964, this figure had only risen by eleven, to 396. These few remnants of a once proud, prosperous, and undefeated nation do not remember their past traditions, obscure when Catlin walked

among them. Their sole distinction now is that of being the
only Indian tribe never to have been at war with the United
States.

Catlin's woes, too, were beginning. Soon after his wife
and family joined him in London, he took his exhibit
throughout the British Isles and onto the continent. And it
was in Paris that—on July 28 of 1845—his beloved wife, now
the mother of four children, died of pneumonia and, perhaps, homesickness.

His deafness increased, soon to be complete.

Audiences slackened. Catlin was, it must be admitted, a
bit too much of a showman for his message to be taken
seriously.

He was tired, very tired. He would sell his collection and
return to full-time painting. He was, after all, an artist, not
an entrepreneur. He wrote to Congress, offering his entire
collection to the United States government for sixty-five
thousand dollars.

While he waited—and waited—for an answer, an epidemic, presumably typhoid, broke out in Paris. All of his
children were stricken and his only son, George, died.

Shortly after this, Catlin was victimized by the French
political situation; specifically, the Revolution of 1848. Officers of the new Republic ransacked his apartment, slashing
their bayonets through his stacked portraits, for it was believed he had been a friend of the deposed king, Louis
Philippe.

Bewildered by the succession of disasters, Catlin took his
three motherless children and his diminished goods back to

London. There he reopened his "Indian Gallery" in a different location; but visitors were few.

His nights and days were devoted to another work, entitled *Notes on Eight Years' Travel and Residence in Europe with Catlin's North American Indian Collection*. It was a miserable book, reflecting its author's growing bitterness and despair. So humiliated was he by the reviews that he hid from everyone for two years.

Then, good news! At last, the House of Representatives had voted to buy his collection for fifty thousand dollars. Of course, he reasoned jubilantly, the bill would pass the Senate. And it would have—except for one vote. Senator Jefferson Davis, a friend of Catlin, opposed it. His Southern constituents desired the Indian lands for themselves, and did not want any sympathy aroused for the Indian cause.

Still more trouble waited in the wings for this star-crossed lawyer-artist-showman. His creditors were pressing him hard. To save his collection, Catlin mortgaged and remortgaged it, and played the stock market. Everything failed, and he was ruined. His "Gallery" was seized and auctioned off in small lots, most of it becoming the property of one Joseph Harrison of Philadelphia.

Even his three daughters were taken away from him by his wife's relatives—wealthy ones, able to give the girls advantages their paupered father could not.

It was almost more than the human spirit could bear.

For some unknown reason, Catlin returned to Paris, where he happened upon a book, *The South American Travels of Baron von Humboldt*. He read and reread it. And, crushed as he was, George Catlin began to dream anew. South America, it would appear, teemed with Indians. He was only fifty-seven years old. He could go there, paint another five or six hundred Indian pictures, and with them redeem his lost "Gallery."

With Catlin, to resolve was to act. During his South American years, he painted incessantly—the Muras, the Maranhas, the Yahuas, the Orejones, the Angosturas, Mayoroones, Iquitos, Omagues, Cocomas, Ticunas, Sepibos, and Chetibos. He thought them ugly and uninteresting, and through it all he longed for the Indians of his own continent.

So, aboard the schooner *Sally Anne*, he journeyed from Lima, Peru, to San Francisco, then on to the Aleutian and Vancouver Islands, painting the Northwest Coast tribes as he went.

No one knows how he raised the fare, but in the spring of 1855, Catlin again sailed for Europe, taking his new Indian pictures with him. He went first to Berlin, to visit in person Baron von Humboldt, now an old, old man. Through the Baron, Catlin was presented to the King and Queen of Prussia, who bought a few of his paintings.

After a brief trip back to South America and another to England, Catlin settled himself in meager lodgings in Brussels. There he retouched and painted from memory and his sketches. He was determined to take back to the United States a second collection of paintings as large as his first, lost one. He did so; but by then he, too, was an old man. His daughters, now independently wealthy, offered him a home, but he refused; he had much work to do—preparing the magnificent exhibition that would reinstate him as the great American artist, and—more important—earn the money to reclaim his "Gallery" from Joseph Harrison.

The new exhibition duly opened in New York City, but
it did not do well. The timing was extremely bad; the Boss
Tweed political scandals had just broken on the news scene,
and no reporter could be bothered with anything so tame
as wild Indians. Then too, P. T. Barnum, circus promoter
extraordinary, had just arrived in town. His lavish adver-
tisements soon forced poor Catlin to concede. *The New
York Times*, in the closing week of November, 1871, carried this brief, stark notice:

THE LAST WEEK
Catlin's Indian Cartoons
Six hundred paintings, with 20,000 figures

What to do, where to go? Just then his old friend from
Albany, Joseph Henry, now Secretary of the Smithsonian
Institution in Washington, D.C., invited him to exhibit
there. Catlin was thrilled; honor was his at last! Henry even
provided him, rent-free, a tiny turret room where he lived,
drew, retouched his works, and wrote endless petitions to
Congress. And here it was that, after realizing that charity
and not honor had prompted Henry's invitation, he became
so weak, so infirm that he had to be taken to Jersey City,
where one of his daughters lived. In the early dawn of
December 23, 1872, crying out, "But what will become of
my Gallery?" George Catlin died.

Long afterward, much—but not all—of his lost collection
was found in the basement of Harrison's boiler factory, in
Philadelphia. Not all of it, for numerous fires and fire hose
drenchings had ruined a portion. Mice had nested in some
artifacts; moths had gorged themselves on feathered head-

dresses and furred robes; picture frames had cracked and warped; canvases had shrunk and split.

Today, safe from further depredation, over four hundred of the full-length portraits of Indians and scenes of Indian life are housed in the Smithsonian National Museum, while most of his sketches—some seven hundred of them—are stored in the American Museum of Natural History in New York City.

The mortal remains of the vision-haunted man who created them lie—quietly, it is hoped—in a rarely visited grave in Green-Wood Cemetery on Long Island, not so very far from his birthplace of Wilkes-Barre; while many hundreds of miles west, on the upper reaches of the Missouri River, where they fell, one by one, victims of one of mankind's worst scourges, lie the Mandan Indians—the Welsh Indians, Catlin said. Strange is the fate that linked together, never to be separated, such an eccentric man and such a singular nation.

CHAPTER 8

From Mobile Bay to the Missouri River

IF PRINCE MADOG
landed his colonists in Mobile Bay in 1171, and if the Mandan Indians, known to be flourishing along the Heart River six hundred years later, were the descendants of those colonists, then we are faced with an obvious question. How did the Welshmen, gradually becoming "Welsh Indians," get from the Gulf of Mexico to the Missouri River? What was their route; and does any proof of it exist?

The evidence for Madog's having ended his long voyage in Mobile Bay—a tablet commemorating his landfall there has been erected at Fort Morgan, Alabama—lies in reasoning plus some, admittedly slight, documentation. If he followed the ocean currents, as he was certain to do, he would have been carried into the Gulf of Mexico. Searching for a suitable landing site, Mobile Bay—then a perfect harbor, ringed by sheltering hills—would surely have attracted him as it did later explorers: Ponce de Leon, Alonzo de Pineda,

Hernando de Soto, and Amerigo Vespucci.

As to the documentation: in 1519, Diego Ribeiro, a Por-
tuguese cartographer in the employ of Spain, drew a map
of the known world with the words *Tierra de los Gales*
(Land of the Welsh) upon a thin line pointing to what is
now called Mobile Bay. At right angles to this line, another
short one points slightly upward—northward. This chart is
now part of the Ibañez Cartographical Collection in Seville,
Spain.

Much later testimony to the landing in Mobile Bay lies in
an exchange of letters between Major Amos Stoddard,
whom we have already met, and John Sevier, frontiersman
and statesman, who fought Indians in the Tennessee Valley
for over thirty years, then served two terms as the first and
third Governor of Tennessee, the state he really brought
into being.

Under date of August 30, 1810, Stoddard wrote to Sevier:

> As I am an utter stranger to you, I should not ven-
> ture to address you on the present occasion, were I not
> in some measure encouraged to do so by your old
> friend, Governor Claiborne, who has just left this
> place.
>
> The object of this communication is to request a
> statement of particulars of a story, which Governor
> Claiborne thinks you detailed to him some years ago.
> According to this account, you once saw an ancient
> book in the hands of a Cherokee woman which you
> supposed was written in the Welsh characters, said to
> be given to her by an Indian from the west side of the
> Mississippi, and which was afterwards burned with
> her house.
>
> I have been some time collecting material to prove

the existence of a Welsh colony on this continent, which landed here, according to the testimony of history, as early as 1170. If you can call to mind the circumstances to which I have alluded, and will be so good as to communicate them to me, I shall feel myself under many obligations to you.

Signed:

AMOS STODDARD, Major
2nd. Corps, U.S.

And from Knoxville, Governor Sevier, who probably knew more about the southeastern Indians than any other white man, replied:

Knoxville, October 9, 1810

Sir,

Your letter of August 30 ult. is before me.

With respect to the information you have requested, I shall with pleasure give you so far as my memory will serve me, aided by a memorandum taken on the subject of a people called the Welsh Indians. In the year 1782 I was on campaign against some part of the Cherokee; during the route I had discovered traces of very ancient, though regular fortifications. Some short time after the expedition I had made, I took the opportunity of inquiring of a venerable old chief called Oconostota, who was then, and had been for nearly sixty years, the ruling chief of the Cherokee Nation, if he could inform me what people it had been which had left such fortifications in their country, and in particular one on the bank of the Highwassee River.

The old Chief immediately informed me: 'It is handed down by the Forefathers that the works had been made by the White people who had formerly inhabited the country now called Carolina; that a war had existed between the two nations for several years. At length it was discovered that the Whites were making a large number of boats which induced the Cherokee to suppose they were about to descend the Tennessee River. They [the Cherokee] then assembled their whole band of warriors and took the shortest and most convenient route to the Muscle Shoals in order to intercept them on their passage down the river. In a few days the boats hove in sight. A warm combat ensued with various success for several days.

'At length the Whites proposed to the Indians that if they would exchange prisoners and cease hostilities, they would leave the country and never return, which was acceded to; and after the exchange they parted friendly. That the Whites then descended the Tennessee down to the Ohio, thence down to the Big River [the Mississippi], then they ascended it up to the Muddy River [the Missouri] and thence up that river for a great distance. They were then on some of its branches, "but," said he, "they are no more White people; they are now all become Indians, and look like other red people of the country." '

I then asked him if he had ever heard any of his ancestors saying what nation of people these Whites belonged to. He answered he "had heard his grandfather and father say they were a people called Welsh, and that they had crossed the Great Water and landed first near the mouth of the Alabama River near Mobile and had been driven up to the heads of the waters until they arrived at Highwassee River."

Many years ago I happened in company with a Frenchman who had lived with the Cherokee and he said that he had formerly been high up the Missouri. He informed me that he had traded with the Welsh tribe; that they certainly spoke much of the Welsh dialect, and though their customs were savage and wild, yet many of them, particularly the females, were very fair and white, and they frequently told him that they had sprung from a nation of White people. He also stated that some scraps of old books remained among them, but in such tattered and destructive order that nothing intelligent remained in the pieces or scraps. He observed their settlement was in an obscure quarter on a branch of the Missouri running through lofty mountains. His name has escaped me.

The chief Oconostota informed me [that] an old woman in his Nation, named Peg, had some part of an old book given her by an Indian living high up in the Missouri, and thought he was one of the Welsh tribe. Unfortunately before I had an opportunity of seeing the book the old woman's house and its contents were consumed by fire. I have conversed with several persons, who saw and examined the book, but it was so worn and disfigured that nothing intelligible remained; neither did any one of them understand any language but their own, and even that, very imperfectly.

I have thus, Sir, communicated and detailed the particulars of your request, so far as I have any information on the subject, and wish it were more comprehensive than you will find written here.

Signed:

JOHN SEVIER

As Sevier indicated, there exist in Alabama, Georgia, and Tennessee at least three heavy stone fortifications which, archaeologists agree, were built a few hundred years before Columbus arrived. It is also agreed that they are totally unlike any known Indian defense works. (The Indians used picket stockades, hastily erected.) All three are thought to be the work of one group of people within a single generation; and it is obvious—because of the tremendous labor

John Sevier, governor of Tennessee

involved—that they were made by a people in deadly peril. Months, maybe years, of toil were required to build each one. What is equally astonishing is the nearly complete preservation of these well-planned and skillfully built forts into this twentieth century.

The three are De Soto Falls Fort, on top of Lookout Mountain, in Alabama; Fort Mountain in Georgia; and Old Stone Fort in Tennessee. These defenses are grouped in a rough triangle on the northward route that, according to Oconostota, the Welsh settlers followed. Presumably, the colonists anchored in the deep water at the lower end of Mobile Bay behind the present Fort Morgan, then came ashore in coracles, perhaps venturing up a small stream originally called Mad Dog (Madog?) River, now known just as Dog River. Their main route, though, would have been up the Alabama, Coosa, and Hiwassee Rivers, or overland along parallel trails worn by buffalo and deer.

Where the Alabama joins the Coosa, in northeastern Alabama near the borders of Georgia and Tennessee, lies Lookout Mountain, part of the Allegheny range, about a thousand feet high and close to De Soto Falls. Here the first of the forts was erected. Unfortunately, during the past several years, this fort has been subject to vandalism; stones have been removed from its walls to build summer cottages and a commercial dam, and about all that remains is a mound covered over with dead leaves. But in 1833, a man named Josiah Priest gave a careful description of De Soto Falls Fort in his book *American Antiquities and Discoveries in the West*:

> The top of the mountain is mostly level. On this range, notwithstanding its height, a river [Little River] has its source, after traversing it for about seventy miles, plunges over a precipice [De Soto Falls]. The rock from which the water falls is circular, and juts over considerably. Immediately below the falls, on each side of the river, are bluffs which rise two hundred feet. Around one of these bluffs the river makes a bend, which forms a peninsula.
>
> On top of this peninsula are the remains of what is esteemed to be fortifications which consist of a stone wall built on the very brow of this tremendous ledge. The whole length of the wall is thirty-seven rods and eight feet, including about two acres of ground.
>
> The only descent from this place is between two

rocks, for about thirty feet, when a bench of the ledge
presents itself, from two to five feet in width and
ninety feet long. This bench is the only road or path
up from the water's edge to the summit. But just at the
foot of the two rocks, where they reach this path, and
within thirty feet of the top of the rock, are five rooms,
which have been formed by dint of great labour. The
entrances of these rooms are very small, but when
within, they are found to communicate with each
other by doors or apertures . . . Twenty men could
have withstood the whole army of Xerxes, as it was
impossible for more than one [man] to pass at a time
and [he] might by the slightest push be hurled 150
feet down the rocks.

Of even more interest is the recent finding, by a Kentucky surveyor, that this fort was nearly identical, in layout
and placement, to Dolwyddelan Castle in Gwynedd, the
supposed birthplace of Madog. Both were equally inacces-
sible, being built atop a high, precipitous rock; both had
small entrances and the same arrangement of ditches or
moats. The same materials and method of construction were
employed: local stones, squared, and held together in a
distinctive pattern by hard mortar.

In cliffs very near the fort are caves with rooms roughly
carved by crude metal tools, proving the caves were inhabited at one time. The obvious suggestion that Hernando
de Soto and his men were responsible for both the fort and
the caves is refuted by the fact that De Soto kept a meticulous day-by-day journal, and no mention is made of any
such activity; rather, he records finding one such fortification. Moreover, in the short time he and his company
camped in the area, it would have been humanly impossi-

De Soto Falls

ble to accomplish this. Also, these are defensive works, and De Soto was always on the offensive.

Presumably harrassed by hostile Indians, the Welshmen in a few years abandoned their mountaintop, and pushed northeast along the Coosa River into present-day Georgia. Again, they built a high bastion; but a little more quickly than before, for these boulders are fitted together without any mortar. The long main wall was erected in a series of angles; each "pit" so formed could shelter up to a half-dozen men. Hughes Reynolds in his *Coosa River Valley* describes Fort Mountain, the name given to this fortification:

> On the top of a peak in the Cohutta Range 2838 feet in height are the remains of a stone wall, 855 feet long, quite evidently built to protect the builders from an invading force. In fact, it is a fortress, for it was built on the only side of the mountain which is scalable. The stones are mostly flat and are now scattered, but it is evident that the wall was, originally, the height of a man's head. At one point there was a gateway which led to a spring. The wall was built with the skill of military engineers with such angles that all parts of the wall could be defended. Such a defensive work was fully up to the standards of early European military science and far beyond the ability of the Indians to construct unaided. Inside the walls are a number of pits from four to eight feet in width.
>
> The Cherokee legend is that it was built by people with pale faces whom the Indians overcame and chased out of the country . . .

Fortunately, Fort Mountain has suffered less destruction throughout the centuries than the other defense works described here; and its continued protection is assured, since some years ago the owner of the mountain deeded it to the state of Georgia in perpetuity. The area is now a state park, with an observation tower at the summit. The walls of the fort, however, are hidden beneath brush and matted vines, and are some distance from the picnic grounds surrounding the tower. Thus, only persons actually searching for the ancient fort will be apt to come upon it.

After being dislodged from Fort Mountain by attacking tribes, the Welsh colonists either began a lengthy retreat or else dug in for a last stand, as witnessed by a ring of rather hastily built forts around what is now Chattanooga. These smaller structures have been destroyed; but good, relatively recent accounts of them exist.

The first of these minor defense works was the one specifically mentioned by Governor Sevier, on the Hiwassee River—Savannah Fort. The nineteenth *Annual Report* (1898) of the U.S. Bureau of Ethnology describes it: "[at] Savannah on the North Bank of the Hiwassee River is a fort of the same name, five miles above Conesauga Creek and Columbus, in Polk County, Tennessee. Here are extensive remains of an ancient settlement and a cemetery and, also, seventy years ago, a square enclosure or 'fort' of undressed stone."

In his book *The Civil and Political History of Tennessee* (1823) Judge John Haywood of that state wrote that there were "five forts in the Chattanooga area which had been built by white people living there before the Indian occupation." He himself had investigated each of the forts and questioned the local Indians. He locates the five: (1) at the mouth of Chickamauga Creek, just outside present-day Chattanooga; (2) on the Tennessee River, at a village named

Dallas, site of the first Hamilton County Court House, a location now covered by Chickamauga Lake; (3) twenty miles from the mouth of Chickamauga Creek; (4) on the Hiwassee River—the one discussed above; and (5) at Pumpkintown. This latter was a favorite name of the Cherokees (*Ei-ya-ga-u-gi* in their tongue) and several villages were so named; the one Haywood refers to was at the present site of Athens, Tennessee.

Finally, after occupying each of these lesser defenses, the Welsh settlers moved on and built their final major bulwark —Old Stone Fort, on the Duck River, at what is now Manchester, Tennessee. This fortification is an irregular triangle, comprising about fifty acres, and is formed by high bluffs along the Duck River's two forks; a wall of stone, flint, and shale, twenty feet high and twenty feet thick; and a moat connecting the two streams. The moat is twelve hundred feet long, up to twenty feet wide, and—in Haywood's day— was twenty feet deep. Like the other two large defenses— De Soto Falls Fort and Fort Mountain—Old Stone Fort is well designed, evidencing engineering skill far beyond the ability of any of the American Indians. In almost all respects

KEY TO MAP

1. Mad Dog River, now Dog River
2. De Soto Falls, Little River, Alabama
3. Fort Mountain, Georgia
4. Savannah Fort, Polk County, Tennessee
5. Pumpkintown (Athens, Tennessee)
6. An ancient fort on the Hiwassee River
7. Fort on the Tennessee River
8. Fort at the mouth of Chickamauga Creek
9. Fort twenty miles from mouth of Chickamauga Creek
10. Old Stone Fort, Manchester, Tennessee

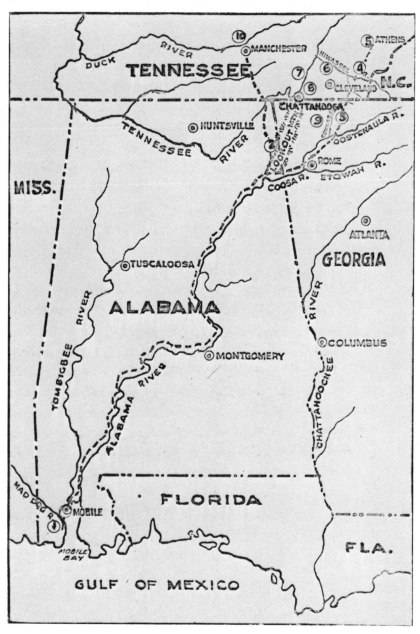

Probable route of the Welsh colonists from Mobile Bay to Old Stone Fort

—siting, arrangement of walls, moat, and single entrance—
these forts are identical to ancient ruins in Wales.

Like the other two, Old Stone Fort has been partially
destroyed—some of the wall material has been removed and
used for road building—but enough remains to show the
original plan. And it has an added distinction: long ago a
hollow in the top of the wall became filled with earth. A
tree, which was cut down in August of 1819, grew in the
hollow. When experts examined the stump, they counted
337 annular rings, proving the wall to have been built sometime—probably a very long time—prior to 1482.

This assumption of a long time is supported by the fact
that well over a hundred years ago, when excavations for
cellars were being made near Old Stone Fort, three Roman
coins were unearthed—two at Manchester, one at Fayette-
ville. A full description of one of the pieces appeared in the
Niles' Weekly Register, a Philadelphia newspaper, on August 22, 1818. After studying this article, a recent secretary of
the American Numismatic Society, Sidney P. Noe, wrote,
"The coin seems to have been a denarius of Antonius Pius.
A piece closely answering the description is in the catalogue
of the British Museum. The coins were of the second century." We know that during the Roman occupation of
Britain coins were minted in Wales; it is entirely possible
that Madog's twelfth-century colonists brought some of
these already ancient coins with them.

After Old Stone Fort the line of defense posts disappears
—except for one in Kentucky—and the trail of the Welshmen becomes difficult to follow. We can only speculate.
One thing seems certain, however: always the Welsh were

defeated; they did not understand Indian-style fighting. As
to their route, the best supposition, with a bit of evidence to
support it, is that the colonists were gradually forced northward into Kentucky, then down the Ohio River, up the
Mississippi to the mouth of the Missouri, then west.

There were countless reports of Welsh Indians in Kentucky. Reuben Durrett, a careful student of American history who devoted nearly a lifetime to the subject of Prince
Madog and his discovery of America, said flatly that tales
of the Welsh Indians were told around every Kentucky
fireside in the eighteenth century. Albert James Pickett, in
his *History of Alabama*, wrote that "there are evident traces
of the Welshmen having formerly inhabited the country
around Kentucky, particularly wells and ruins of buildings,
neither of which was the work of Indians." Still another
Kentuckian, Colonel Bennett H. Young, reported in his *Prehistoric Kentucky* that "a remarkable prehistoric stone fortification in the state of Kentucky is situated in Madison
County about three miles east of Berea. This fort occupies
what is known as Indian Fort Mountain. For the military
skill displayed in the selection of this mountain as a strong-
hold and for the patience and labour expended in building
the necessary walls to render it impregnable, too much cannot be said in praise of both the genius and the skill of the
men who constructed the fortifications. The old forts in
Kentucky were not built by Indians, but by a past people
greatly skilled in arts."

From this last fort, the trail would seem to lead—still
northward—to Sand Island, at the Falls of the Ohio River,
by present-day Louisville. It would appear that the Welshmen lived there peaceably for quite some time. George

Rogers Clark, the explorer and much older brother of William Clark, who moved—with his family—as a lad of fourteen to this site, maintained all his life that the Welshmen had indeed once been there. George Catlin, too, was sure of this:

> ... but this much I can safely aver, that at the moment I first saw these people [the Mandan Indians] I was so struck with the peculiarity of their appearance, that I was under the instant conviction that they were an amalgam of a native with some civilized race; and from what I have seen of them and of the remains of the Missouri and Ohio rivers, I feel fully convinced that these people have emigrated from the latter stream; and that they have . . . with many of their customs, been preserved from the almost total destruction of the bold colonists of Madawc, who, I believe, settled upon and occupied for a century or so, the rich and fertile banks of the Ohio.

But again, there were clashes between the Welsh and the local Indians, culminating in a tremendous battle at the Falls, in which great numbers of the whites were slain. Writing of this, Durrett records that in 1799 six skeletons, wearing brass breastplates engraved with a design reminiscent of the Welsh coat of arms, were dug up at Jeffersonville, near the Falls, on the Indian side of the river. Also, that a tombstone, or part of one, bearing the date 1186, was uncovered there. If so, this—along with the breastplates—has long since vanished.

As recently as 1932, two writers on the archaeology of Jefferson County, W. D. Funkhouser and W. S. Webb, in commenting on the fight at the Falls said:

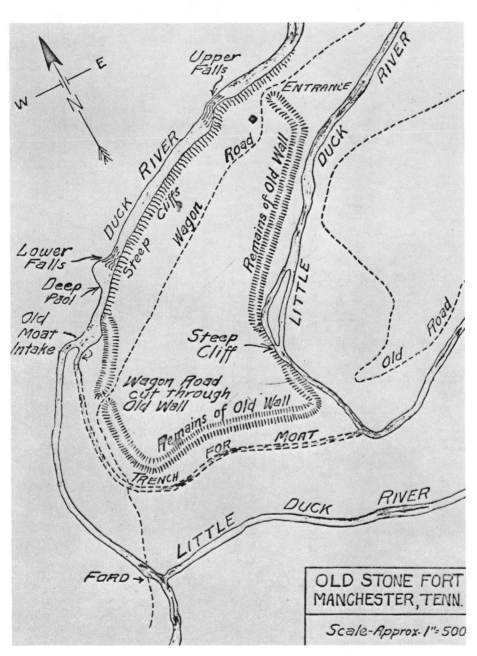

Plat of Old Stone Fort

Whatever archaeological sites Jefferson County may
have had, have long since been obliterated by the
progress of civilization. This is particularly true since
the more important of these sites would probably have
been along the Ohio River, and a large area of the
river front is now occupied by the city of Louisville
and its suburbs. This part of the river is of course asso-
ciated with the well known and oft repeated tradition
of the "White Indians" and the famous battle at the
"Falls of the Ohio" at which the supposed white race
was wiped out of existence.

Yet Sand Island has not been "obliterated by the progress
of civilization." It is still an uninhabited, tree-covered bar
of land in the Ohio River. But so far no archaeologist has
dug to recover the skeletons, armor, and weapons of the
"White Indians," applying to them the Carbon-14 method
of dating, based on radioactive decay, that would let the
world know how long the Welsh colonists have been sleep-
ing there. Perhaps, some day this will be done.

And surely the "White Indians" were not "wiped out of
existence" in this encounter, terrible though the slaughter
was. What of the few who survived? Did they flee—even as
Oconostota said—down the Ohio, up the Mississippi, and
far out the Missouri River, there to grow in numbers and
prosperity, and to await the arrival—several centuries later
—of John Evans, of George Catlin, and of the smallpox. Was
it there, on the bleak prairie, so distant in time and miles
from the sunny shores of Mobile Bay, that the men from
the green hills of Wales fought their final battle and suffered their last defeat?

 CHAPTER 9

Madog in Mexico?

WE HAVE NOW COME
full circle, and end where we began: with Madog himself.
A legend persists that on his second, colonizing voyage, the
Welsh prince and a few of his company became separated,
presumably by accident, from the main group; then, instead
of proceeding north, he and his men followed a southwestern course, into Mexico. The tradition further maintains
that the white, bearded god of the Toltecs, Quetzalcoatl,
was none other than Prince Madog of Wales!

Robert Southey, a poet-laureate of England, featured this
belief in his epic poem, *Madoc*, published in 1805. Other,
less noted, writers have held the same opinion. And while
there seems to be only some slight, circumstantial evidence
to support this claim, we should, in fairness, listen to the
argument.

About the year 1000, the Toltecs, an Indian people who
had come to the Mexican plateau centuries earlier, began
to enlarge their boundaries by forays into surrounding

123

Mayan territory. By the twelfth century they achieved political domination, and their civilization, built upon the earlier Olmec culture, had reached its peak. Their capital was at Tollán, now called Tula in the state of Hidalgo, with other centers at Teotihuacán and Cholula.

The most important person in Toltec history was Quetzalcoatl. This name, Quetzalcoatl, meaning Plumed Serpent, was actually the title of the highest priest and king, and was applied to different men at different times, making for considerable confusion. (It was evidently used much as the Roman emperors had used the title Caesar: Caius Julius Caesar, Augustus Caesar, Lucius Julius Caesar.)

According to the legend, the Quetzalcoatl we are interested in—a historic figure, only later deemed a god—appeared in the east with a company of attendants. A big white man with a beard, he and his men had come over the sea from the north in a square-sailed boat. As was pointed out earlier, no sketches of twelfth-century Welsh ships survive, but from written descriptions in ancient port records in Wales, it is clear that some of the vessels of this period did indeed have square-masted sails. However, ships of other nations may well have carried them, too.

Landing, Quetzalcoatl—or Madog—proceeded to the uplands of Mexico, becoming increasingly dismayed at the Toltec religious ceremonies, which included human sacrifice, sun worship, and a sacred ball game called *tlachtli*. Apparently, Quetzalcoatl and his followers stayed in the country some twenty years in all, preaching peace—Madog had left home searching for peace—and teaching the Indians much, particularly about architecture. True it is that many buildings in Mexico date from 1200, about the time

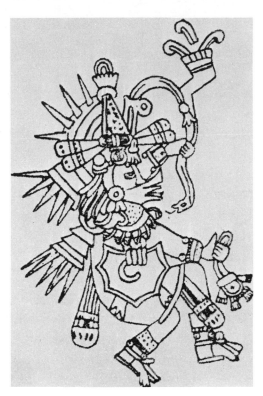

One of the numerous representations of the god Quetzalcoatl, the Plumed Serpent

that Madog could have been in the country; and from the invading Romans, the Welsh had early learned how to make good roads, lay out towns, and erect substantial dwellings.

In Cholula, Quetzalcoatl was able to stop—or greatly lessen—the appalling human sacrifice, persuading the natives to offer their gods bread and flowers and incense instead. After many years, Quetzalcoatl left Cholula and went to Coatzacoalcos (Puerto Mexico). And here it was that this man, now believed to be a god, sailed away—some say on a raft—leaving behind a few of his trusted followers;

but promising them, and the Indians, that he would return one day.

Gradually, the Toltec nation declined and disappeared, destroyed by recurring famine, pestilence, intertribal warfare, and conquest from the north. Many of the Toltecs migrated southward, possibly into Central America; those who remained merged with the northern invaders to create the Chichimec culture. This, in turn, was followed by the composite, highly advanced Aztec civilization.

Through these successive cultures, belief held firm that Quetzalcoatl, the fair god, the Plumed Serpent, would come back. And, through one of the strange coincidences of history, this essentially mystic belief brought about the destruction of the Aztec empire. In 1519, a white, bearded man with a company of attendants again appeared in the east! But this was no mild Welsh prince, seeking peace; it was a Spaniard, Hernando Cortez, bent on conquest. And Montezuma, the despotic, superstitious Aztec emperor, convinced the prophecy was fulfilled—that Cortez and his nearly seven hundred ironclad soldiers, dragging ten large, noisy cannon, were Quetzalcoatl and his men returned—received them graciously at his capital, Tenochtitlán (Mexico City) on November 18. Cortez seized his opportunity; he took Montezuma hostage, and attempted to govern the country through him, meanwhile conspiring with the emperor's many enemies. Too late, Montezuma saw his mistake; but events were moving rapidly to a climax.

In the spring of the following year, 1820, Diego de Velázquez, first Governor of Cuba and Cortez' superior, jealous of his subordinate's easy victory, sent against him a detach-

The Royal Badge of Wales, showing the national emblem, the winged Red Dragon

ment of about a thousand men, led by Pánfilo de Narváez. Somehow learning of this, and leaving Pedro de Alvarado in command at Tenochtitlán, Cortez hastened to the coast to meet, and promptly defeat, this force.

Meanwhile, at Tenochtitlán, Alvarado impetuously massacred many Aztecs, and shortly after Cortez' return the Indians revolted and besieged the Spanish. A battle ensued, and Montezuma was killed; but the Spaniards were routed. On June 30, the famous *noche triste* (dismal night), the Spanish abandoned the city, and retired to Tlaxcala. The following summer, though, Cortez and his army again marched on the capital and, after a three-month siege, Tenochtitlán fell on August 13, 1521. And with it fell the Aztec empire.

Who *was* Quetzalcoatl? That a white, bearded, European man came to Mexico long before the days of Columbus is well documented, and cannot be denied. One of the stronger evidences of this is the statement of the conquering Spaniards themselves, who certainly had nothing to gain by telling the truth. Yet they insisted that when they arrived in Mexico they found traces of Christianity, together with such artifacts as the Cross, among the Indians. But whether these were brought to the country by Madog of Wales, a stray Viking, or some other adventurer, will probably never be known.

Yet the figure of a serpent with quetzal feathers, the symbol of the god Quetzalcoatl, is prominent throughout Mexico today, especially in its art and architecture. One theory is that this design may have developed from a signet ring, embossed with a griffin, which Madog, as a nobleman, is sure to have worn and used, for the griffin, or dragon, was adopted by the ancient Britons as a standard long before the coming of the Saxons. And while dragons are of many kinds—flying dragons, water dragons, fire-breathing dragons, and others—they are essentially reptilian; all have a basic serpent structure upon which the variations in anatomy are superimposed. *Y Ddraig Goch* (the Red Dragon) of Wales, the country's national emblem, is, then, a plumed serpent: it has an eagle's head (except for visible, erect ears); a huge, scaly, winged body with four legs and claws;

a long, looped, barbed tail at one end and a long, spear-pointed tongue at the other.

We know that the most ancient mythologies of the Old World include winged serpents. A fine pair of them drew the chariot of Demeter, the Greek goddess of harvest and fertility. And visitors to the Berlin Museum may see some handsome ones carved on an ancient, undated stone sarcophagus. But had a New World Indian, in the remote highlands of Mexico, in the twelfth century, ever seen or heard of such? Where did the Toltec idea of a winged serpent come from? Was it from a white, bearded man, wearing a signet ring, who came over the sea from Wales?

Unveiling of marker at Fort Morgan in Alabama on November 10, 1953. From left: the late Mrs. Yale Williams, a descendant of an ancient king of Gwynedd; the late Hatchett Chandler, Custodian and Historian of Fort Morgan, who devoted years to the study of Prince Madog and his landing in Mobile Bay; and the late Zella Armstrong, Historian of Hamilton County, Tennessee.

Epilogue

THIS, THEN, HAS been the story of Prince Madog of Wales and his alleged discovery of America in 1170; and of the reports—rife throughout the late seventeenth, eighteenth, and early nineteenth centuries—of the existence of a tribe (or tribes) of Welsh-speaking Indians. It is the story of the searches made for this unique nation, and an examination of the clues to the route the Welsh settlers may have taken, from their landing in Mobile Bay to their extinction, many centuries later, on the upper reaches of the Missouri River.

That it all happened just as set forth is unlikely; that none of it occurred seems equally unlikely. Too many people witnessed *something*. The fact that no official expedition ever proved the Welsh Indians' existence does not, on the other hand, disprove it. And tomorrow—or the day after—someone, somewhere, may happen upon an old manuscript, a piece of armor, an inscription—much as the Reverend Synnott bought, all unwittingly, the ancient port records. Perhaps then we will know for sure whether or not Madog landed in America and left behind him, with the Indians, the Welsh language.

NOTES TO THE CHAPTERS

CHAPTER 1

P. 5 Owain's body was later moved outside the Cathedral, for when Baldwin, Archbishop of Canterbury from 1185 to 1190, came to Bangor while on a tour of Wales exhorting the people to support the Crusades, he ordered the Bishop of Bangor to remove Owain's remains from the Cathedral. The Bishop reluctantly obeyed, but made a passageway from the emptied vault through the building's south wall, and placed Owain's body just outside, yet well within consecrated ground.

P. 8 See Joan Dane's *Prince Madog, Discoverer of America: A Legendary Story.*

P. 8 *Brut y Tywysogyon.* Peniarth ms. 20, copiwyd a golgwyd gyda Rhagymadrodd gan Thomas Jones. Caerdydd: Gwasg Prifysgol Cymru, 1941.

P. 8 *Annales Cambriae, ab A.D. circiter 444 ad usque A.D. 1066.* London: G. E. Eyre & W. Spottiswoode, 1848.

P. 9 See Stephen W. Williams' *The Cistercian Abbey of Strata Florida.* London: Whiting & Company, 1889.

P. 9 The heading reads: *Vita Griffini, filii Conani, Regis venodotiae vel Northwalliae, a thelwello jurisperito Meredithi Latine versa: filio Oweni Gwynedd, et eius navigatione terras incognitas; Wallice.*

P. 12 Richard Hakluyt. *The Principal Navigations, Voiages, Traffiqves and Discoueries of the English Nation.* London: George Bishop, Ralph Newberie and Robert Barker, 1598-1600. 3 v.

P. 12 Samuel Purchas. *Purchas His Pilgrimes.* London: Printed by W. Stansby for H. Fetherstone, 1625. 4 v.

P. 12 John Smith. *The Generall Historie of Virginia, New-England, and the Summer Isles.* London: Printed by I. D. and I. H. for Michael Sparkes, 1624.

P. 12 William H. Prescott. *History of the Conquest of Mexico, with a Preliminary View of the Ancient Mexican Civilization, and the Life of the Conqueror, Hernando Cortes.* Chicago: Hooper, Clarke & Company, 1843. 3 v.

P. 12 John Clark Ridpath. *History of the United States from Aboriginal Times to the Present Day.* New York: H. G. Allen, 1899. 4 v.

P. 12 Benjamin F. De Costa. *The Pre-Columbian Discovery of Amer-*

132

ica. 3rd ed., rev. Albany, New York: J. Munsell's Sons, 1901.

P. 12 This romance, seemingly very popular in its day, is now lost to us. In the prologue to his best known work, *Van den Vos Reinaerde*, the author introduces himself as "Willem, die Madocke makede"; i.e., Willem, who wrote Madoc.

P. 14 Antonio de Arredondo. *Historical Proof of Spain's Title to Georgia: A Contribution to the History of One of the Spanish Borderlands.* Edited by Herbert E. Bolton. Berkeley: University of California Press, 1925.

CHAPTER 2

P. 18 The Welsh text, cited by E. D. Jones in the *Journal of the National Library of Wales,* vol. 14, summer 1965, p. 123, reads: "Madauc ap Ouain Guyned oed vori / ur maur a chuannoc i drafel / ac am na ale o vod aral enkarvtrio / ir Sygned guneuthwr ac adei / lad a unaeth long heb hayarn / ond i hoylio a chyrn / rhac lyncku or mor hunnu hi ai ga / lu oi guneuthuriad Guennan Gorn ac un honno i nofiod y moroed urth i blesser ac i tra- / faeliod lauer o uledyd tra / more yn diarsuyd on urth dymchuelyd adre ynn gyfagos at ynys yr yakyttiod phryd- / ie yno ynn greulon ac ai hamhared ymhel ac an hynny vyth hyd hediu i geluir y mann hunnu ar y mor Phrydie Kasuennann. Yr ystori honn a doeth o lau buy gilyd dann uarant gredad o hynny hyd hediu hediu / Vely i dyvod Eduart ap Sion uynn i mi 1582 y 13 Vis Maurth."

P. 20 See the accounts of Dr. Bombard's voyage in *Time* Magazine, vol. 61, January 5, 1953, p. 28f, and *Senior Scholastic,* vol. 61, January 14, 1953, p. 19.

P. 23 Thomas Stephens. *Madoc: An Essay on the Discovery of America by Madoc ab Owain Gwynedd.* London: Longmans, Green & Company, 1893.

P. 25 See *Welsh Histories and Poets,* 1796.

P. 28 See the account in Richard Deacon's *Madoc and the Discovery of America: Some New Light on an Old Controversy.* New York: George Braziller, 1966, pp. 98-100.

CHAPTER 3

P. 31 *The Relation of David Ingram . . . of Sundry Things Which He . . . Did See in Travelling by Land from the Most Northerly Part of the Bay of Mexico . . . Through a Great Part of America . . . Which He Reported . . . in August and September, 1582.* A reprint of this can be found in volume 5 of Edward Arber's *An English Garner: Ingatherings from Our History and Literature.* Westminster: A. Constable and Company, 1880-1897. 8 v.

P. 32 This letter was later given by Dr. Lloyd to Edward Llwyd, Keeper of the Ashmolean Museum at Oxford.

P. 34 See *Gentleman's Magazine,* vol. 61, 1791.

P. 34 The Chrochan letter is dated August 24, 1753, and is reprinted in Amos Stoddard's *Sketches, Historical and Descriptive, of Louisiana,* and in George Burder's *The Welch Indians.*

P. 37   Regarding Chaplain, see John Filson in his *The Discovery, Settlement, and Present State of Kentucke.* Wilmington, Delaware: Printed by James Adams, 1784.

P. 38   Major Amos Stoddard. *Sketches, Historical and Descriptive, of Louisiana.* Philadelphia: Mathew Carey, 1812.

P. 39   Some accounts give the name as Maurice Griffiths; Griffith would appear to be correct.

CHAPTER 4

P. 47-48   Quoted from William Owen-Pughe's report, published in the *Gentleman's Magazine,* vol. 61, 1791.

CHAPTER 5

P. 60   It is not difficult to find descriptions of this colorful Omaha chief. See John Bradbury, *Travels in the Interior of America, in the Years 1809, 1810, and 1811.* London: Sherwood, Neely and Jones, 1817. Bradbury ascended the Missouri River in company with the Pacific Fur Company's expedition in 1811, under command of Wilson P. Hunt. See also Truteau's journal, reprinted in the *American Historical Review,* vol. 19, 1914, pp. 299-333.

P. 62   The Mackay Notes are in the archives of the Missouri Historical Society. Paraphrases of Mackay's instructions to Evans can be found in many sources; among them are the *American Historical Review,* vol. 54, 1949, pp. 277-295 and 508-529; the *Missouri Historical Review,* vol. 25, 1931, pp. 219-239, 442-460, and 585-608; Hartmann's *Americans from Wales,* and Williams' *John Evans a Chwedl Madog.*

P. 65   *Hudson's Bay Company Archives,* B. 22/2/4, Brandon House Journal, under date April 14, 1797.

P. 66   David Williams. *John Evans a Chwedl Madog,* 1770-1799. Caerdydd: Gwasg Prifysgol Cymru, 1963.

P. 68-69   Deacon, *op. cit.,* p. 148.

P. 69   *Reglamentos de Don Manuel Gayoso de Lemos,* New Orleans, 1797. The Gayoso papers are in the Archivo General de Indias in Seville, Spain.

CHAPTER 6

P. 71   Benjamin F. Lewis. "The Madog Tradition: the Search for the Madogians, and Other Incidents in the Welsh History of Utica, Past and Present," in *Transactions* of the Oneida Historical Society, no. 6. 1892/94, pp. 117-135.

P. 72   The Stoddard title is cited in Benjamin F. Lewis' article, cited directly above. Evidently, this is Lewis' error, as no such title by Stoddard can be identified. Mrs. Goldena Howard, Reference Librarian at the State Historical Society of Missouri, which houses the Stoddard archives, believes it a misquote for his *Sketches, Historical and Descriptive, of Louisi-*

ana. So does Christine I. Andrew, Senior Reference Librarian at Yale University Library.

CHAPTER 7

P. 82   A good, brief resume of the early visits of white men to the Mandans, and of the Mandan culture, is: G. F. Will and H. J. Spinden. *The Mandans: A Study of Their Culture, Archaeology, and Language.* Cambridge: Museum of American Archaeology and Ethnology, Harvard University, 1906.

P. 87   In the *Missouri Historical Review*, vol. 17, April 1923, p. 345, Frederick Steines cites a rare book about Missouri by a certain Mr. von Martels: *Letters Concerning the Western Part of the United States of America, by Heinrich von Martels, 1st Lieutenant of the 8th Royal Hanoverian Battalion.* Osnabruck: 1834. In 1832 von Martels had sailed for America, and settled in Missouri. In 1833, he returned to his native land and published his book. He later returned to America, but under date of January 30, 1833, he wrote in a letter, ". . . at Gen. Clark's who is in charge of Indian affairs, I saw several Ottos from the upper Missouri. Gen. Clark's museum contains many Indian curiosities, the greater part of which he gathered in the years 1804-6, when he and Captain Lewis and forty companions explored the Louisiana Purchase. When the seventy-year-old Gen. Clark spoke of the daughters of the Mandan his eyes beamed with youthful fire and he answered me that they were the handsomest women in the world . . ." Steines says that at the time of his writing, 1923, a copy of von Martels' book was in the Belleville, Illinois, Public Library.

P. 88   Henry M. Brackenridge. *Journal of a Voyage Up the River Missouri.* 2nd ed. Baltimore: 1816. pp. 178-179.

P. 88   George Catlin. *Letters and Notes on the Manners, Customs, and Condition of the North American Indian.* London: Egyptian Hall, Piccadilly, 1842.

P. 90   Hjalmar Rued Holand. "Oldest Native Document in America," *Journal of American History*, vol. 4, 1910, p. 184, note.

P. 92   Catlin, *op. cit.*

P. 93   *Ibid.*

P. 94   Maximilian, Prince of Wied. *Travels in the Interior of North America.* Translated from the German by H. Evans Lloyd. London: Ackermann and Company, 1843.

P. 98   James Girty. "A Welsh-Indian Vocabulary." Manuscript. Extracts made from this by a Thomas C. Pritchard of Harrisburg, Pennsylvania, in 1789, are among the *Papers* of Peter Burrell, Baron Gwydyr.

CHAPTER 8

P. 107   Governor Claiborne was William Clark Cole Claiborne, 1775-1817, who was successively governor of the Mississippi Territory (1801-1804), the Orleans Territory (1804-1812), and Louisiana (1812-1816).

P. 110   Judge Samuel Cole Williams of Tennessee said that this Frenchman was Francis Budwine. According to Williams, sometime between 1730 and 1735 a band of Cherokee on an expedition on the Mississippi River, overcame a French boat and took the crew prisoners. Among the men was Francis Budwine, who afterward lived with the Cherokee for a time. This name is probably the American corruption of François Boudouin.

P. 110 Both Stoddard's letter of inquiry and Sevier's reply are in the Ayers Collection in the Newberry Library, in Chicago.

P. 114 The Kentucky surveyor was Mr. Arthur F. Griffiths. See Deacon, *op. cit.*, p. 203.

P. 115 Hughes Reynolds. *The Coosa River Valley from De Soto to Hydroelectric Power*. Cynthiana, Ky.; The Hobson Book Press, 1944.

P. 119 See Zella Armstrong. *Who Discovered America? The Amazing Story of Madog*.

P. 120 Reuben T. Durrett. *Traditions of the Earliest Visits of Foreigners to North America, the First Formed and First Inhabited of the Continents*. Louisville: J. P. Morton & Company, printers to the Filson Club, 1908.

P. 120 Albert James Pickett. *History of Alabama, and Incidentally of Georgia and Mississippi, from the Earliest Period*. 3rd ed. Charleston, S. C.: Walker and James, 1851, 2 v. The *History* closes with the death in 1820 of William W. Bibb, first governor of the state of Alabama.

P. 120 Colonel Bennett H. Young. *The Prehistoric Men of Kentucky*. Louisville: J. P. Morton & Company, printers to the Filson Club, 1910.

P. 122 Catlin, *op. cit.*

P. 122 W. D. Funkhouser and W. S. Webb. *Archaeological Survey of Kentucky*. Lexington: Department of Anthropology and Archaeology, University of Kentucky, 1932.

CHAPTER 9

P. 124 The facts given here are to be found in any standard history of Mexico, up to 1519, such as Frederick A. Peterson's *Ancient Mexico: An Introduction to the Pre-Hispanic Cultures*. New York: Putnam, 1959. See also: George C. Vaillant. *Aztecs of Mexico: Origin, Rise and Fall of the Aztec Nation*. Garden City, N.Y.: Doubleday, Doran & Company, Inc., 1941.

SELECTED BIBLIOGRAPHY

Additional detailed references will be found in the Notes to the Chapters

Armstrong, Zella. *Who Discovered America? The Amazing Story of Madog.* Chattanooga: The Lookout Publishing Company, 1950.

Blackwell, Henry. "Madoc and His Discovery of America." *Cambrian,* volume X, November, 1890, pp. 324-326.

Boland, Charles Michael. *They All Discovered America.* New York: Doubleday & Company, Inc., 1961. Chapter XVI.

Bowen, Benjamin F. *America Discovered by the Welsh in 1170 A.D.* Philadelphia: J. B. Lippincott & Company, 1876.

Bradbury, John. *Travels in the Interior of America, in the Years 1809, 1810, and 1811.* London: Sherwood, Neely and Jones, 1817.

Brown, John P. *Old Frontiers: The Story of the Cherokee Indians from Earliest Times to the Date of Their Removal to the West, 1838.* Kingsport, Tennessee: Southern Publishers, Inc., 1938.

Burder, George. *The Welch Indians; or a Collection of Papers Respecting a People whose Ancestors Emigrated from Wales to America in the Year 1170, with Prince Madoc, and Who Are Said Now to Inhabit a Beautiful Country on the West Side of the Mississippi.* London: Printed for T. Chapman, 1797.

Catlin, George. *Letters and Notes on the Manners, Customs, and Condition of the North American Indian.* 2 vols. London: Egyptian Hall, Piccadilly, 1842.

Dane, Joan. *Prince Madog, Discoverer of America: A Legendary Story.* London: Elliott Stock, 1909.

Deacon, Richard. *Madoc and the Discovery of America: Some New Light on an Old Controversy.* New York: George Braziller, 1966.

de Arrendondo, Antonio. *Historical Proof of Spain's Title to Georgia: a Contribution to the History of One of the Spanish Borderlands.* Edited by Herbert E. Bolton. Berkeley: University of California Press, 1925.

De Costa, Benjamin F. *The Pre-Columbian Discovery of America.* 3rd edition, rev. Albany, New York: J. Munsell's Sons, 1901.

Durrett, Reuben F. *Traditions of the Earliest Visits of Foreigners to North America, the First Formed and First Inhabited of the Continents.* Louisville, Kentucky: J. P. Morgan & Company, printers to the Filson Club, 1908.

Evans, E. "Madog ab Owain." *Cambrian,* vol. III, September-October, 1883, pp. 232-234.

Filson, John. *The Discovery, Settlement, and Present State of Kentucke.* Wilmington, Delaware: Printed by James Adams, 1784.

Greenwood, Isaac J. "The Rev. Morgan Jones and the Welsh Indians of Virginia." *New England Historical and Genealogical Register,* LII, January, 1898, pp. 28-36.

Haberly, Loyd. *Pursuit of the Horizon: A Life of George Catlin.* New York: The Macmillan Company, 1948.

Hakluyt, Richard. *The Principal Navigations, Voiages, Traffiqves and Discoueries of the English Nation.* 3 volumes. London: George Bishop, Ralph Newberie, and Robert Barker, 1598-1600.

Hartmann, Edward G. *Americans from Wales.* Boston: Christopher Publishing House, 1967.

Herbert, Sir Thomas. *A Relation of Some Yeares' Travaile.* London: William Stansby, 1634.

Holand, Hjalmar R. *Explorations in America Before Columbus.* New York: Twayne Publisher, 1956.

Lloyd, Sir John Edward. *A History of Wales from the Earliest Times to the Edwardian Conquest.* 3rd ed., 2 vols. London: Longmans, Green and Company, Ltd., 1939.

Maximilian, Prince of Wied. *Travels in the Interior of North America.* Translated from the German by H. Evans Lloyd. London: Ackermann & Company, 1843.

McCracken, Harold. *George Catlin and the Old Frontier.* New York: Dial Press, 1959.

Nasatir, A. P. "John Evans, Explorer and Surveyor." *Missouri Historical Review,* Vol. XXV, 1931, pp. 219-239; 432-460; 585-608.

Prescott, William H. *History of the Conquest of Mexico, with a Preliminary View of the Ancient Mexican Civilization, and the Life of the Conqueror, Hernando Cortes.* 3 vols. Chicago: Hooper, Clarke & Company, 1843.

Purchas, Samuel. *Purchas His Pilgrimes.* 4 vols. London: Printed by W. Stansby for H. Fetherstone, 1625.

Reynolds, Hughes. *The Coosa River Valley from De Soto to Hydroelectric Power.* Cynthiana, Kentucky: The Hobson Book Press, 1944.

Ridpath, John Clark. *History of the United States from Aboriginal Times to the Present Day.* 4 vols. New York: H. C. Allen, 1899.

Smith, John. *The Generall Historie of Virginia, New-England, and the Summer Isles.* London: Printed by I. D. and I. H. for Michael Sparkes, 1624.

Stephens, Thomas. *Madoc: An Essay on the Discovery of America by Madoc ab Owain Gwynedd.* London: Longmans, Green & Company, 1893.

Stoddard, Major Amos. *Sketches, Historical and Descriptive, of Louisiana.* Philadelphia: Mathew Carey, 1812.

Will, G. F. and Spinden, H. J. *The Mandans: A Study of Their Culture, Archaeology and Language.* Cambridge, Massachusetts: Peabody Museum of American Archaeology and Ethnology, Harvard University, 1906. (*Papers,* vol. 3, no. 4.)

Williams, David. *John Evans a Chwedl Madog, 1770-1799.* Caerdydd: Gwasg Prifysgol Cymru, 1963.

———. "John Evans' Strange Journey." *American Historical Review,* vol. LIV, 1949, pp. 277-295; 508-529.

INDEX